THE

girlfriend
TEST

THE
girlfriend
TEST

A Quiz for Women Who Want to Be a Better Date and a Better Mate

WENDY L. WALSH, M.A.

THREE RIVERS PRESS • NEW YORK

Published by Three Rivers Press, New York, New York.
Member of the Crown Publishing Group, a division of Random House, Inc.

www.randomhouse.com

THREE RIVERS PRESS and the Tugboat design are registered trademarks of Random House, Inc.

Printed in the United States of America

Library of Congress Cataloging-in-Publication Data

Walsh, Wendy (Wendy-Lee)
    The girlfriend test : a quiz for women who want to be a better date and a better mate /
Wendy L. Walsh.—1st ed.
    1. Dating (Social customs).   2. Man-woman relationships.   3. Single men—Attitudes.
4. Single women—Psychology.   5. Personality tests. I. Title.
    HQ801.W277   2002
    646.7'7—dc21

    2002010142

ISBN 0-609-80941-5

10   9   8   7   6   5   4   3   2   1

First Edition

To the object of my anxious
attachment —
The feelings you ignite in me
helped immensely with this book.

acknowledg- ments

An author would not be an author without an agent and an editor. Those two humans take a writer's notion and direct it toward something people might actually read. Thanks again to Carrie Thornton at Three Rivers Press and Jan Miller at Dupree/Miller for keeping the team tight and efficient for round number two.

Where would a woman be without other women with whom to laugh, cry, and complain (also known as bitch and moan)? My group includes Dr. Zari Hedayat, Jodie Fisher, Ilsa Glanzberg, Lora McLaughlin, and Debra Snell. I *love* you guys.

When I hunker at my computer or charge through graduate school or run around to TV sets, I have another estrogen alliance keeping the rest of my life and body from tumbling into chaos—my thanks go to Monique Zeno, Robin Mintz, Lisa Morales, Robert Raphael (honorary member of the girls' club),

Michelle Berryhill, Elyse Carey, Ana Santos Huertas, and Blanca Orozco.

David Mirkin's welcome contribution to this book is the loan of an ergonomic seat to ease my aching neck. It now has a heart-shaped impression of my ass on it. Do you still want it back, Dave?

A special thanks to Henry Schleiff at Court TV, Kevin Meagher at Popular Arts Entertainment, and Dr. Marvin Koven at California Graduate Institute for being patient when my life as an author gets in the way of my life as a TV host or student.

Virgil McDowell and Carrington McDowell-Walsh provide my reason for being. And, I wouldn't be a writer if I weren't a mother. The two roles are mysteriously intertwined. My angel daughter gives me jewels of four-year-old wisdom every day. Today's quote is, "If you're looking at someone else, you can't see yourself." So true, my love. That's why I wrote *The Girlfriend Test*.

contents

prologue

I am a woman. I am a mother. I have
a master's degree in psychology.
I am a journalist. I am a girlfriend.
Does that make me an expert in
human relations?

I can't tell you how excited I am to sit down and begin my
second book. As many of you know, my first book, *The
Boyfriend Test,* was a cathartic experience for me, a chance to
examine my own choices in men and document them along the
way. I used lessons from the fields of psychology, anthropology,
and biology and applied them to real-life dating stories—my
own and those of other women from many walks of life. The
result was a very personal and sometimes humorous book that
thousands of people related to.

It was also an emotional risk for me. I received many, many
e-mails in response. Fortunately the vast majority of you who
read my first book told me how much in common we all have,
thanked me for my observations, and then blessed me with
forgiveness for my foibles. The hard part for me was dealing
with the few people who took my stories of relationship failures

as a sign of weakness rather than wisdom. Fortunately, there were those smart, observant folks (men and women alike) who simply remarked on my bravery in "putting myself out there." I really feel blessed to have those empathetic people on the planet. And I thank everyone for taking the time to read my words. The positive feedback gave me the courage to try this again. But the negative feedback helped me grow the most. Thanks to you all.

I began my last book with a famous quote from the novel *Illusions: The Adventures of a Reluctant Messiah,* by Richard Bach. The quote was: "We teach best what we most need to learn." The principles behind such wisdom are simple. When we need to learn a new skill, we do two things: We break it down into small, easily performed components. And then we practice them over and over until we can put all the pieces together and finally get it right. So who would you rather take lessons from? The person who is effortlessly and unconsciously skilled or one who has analyzed the technique and continues to practice her way to competence?

Put in an example we can all relate to, if you hired a personal trainer to help you lose weight, would you prefer the Barbie at the gym with the ectomorph physique, "normal" eating habits, and natural athletic ability or the woman who lost 40 pounds herself, has worked hard at the gym for years to keep it off, and has a few tips for surviving eating binges and couch-potato stints? My money is on the hard worker. Because . . . we teach best what we most need to learn.

Now I am still learning to be a better girlfriend. I am not a veteran of a twenty-five-year union who has found relationships easy. I've always felt that duration is a strange litmus test for relationship quality, anyway. I am that trainer at the gym who is working hard in a conscious way to connect with her clients. I still make some mistakes, but I keep getting better at being authentic and honest. And I'd like to take you along for the ride to share some of my newfound knowledge—as I work hard to grow. I know you'll understand, girlfriend.

"The greatest thing you'll ever learn is
just to love, and be loved in return."

Eben Ahbez, from the song "Nature Boy"

intro-
duction

> An attachment injury is an
> abandonment or betrayal of trust
> during a critical moment of need.
> S. M. JOHNSON, J. A. MAKINEN,
> AND J. W. MILLIKIN, JOURNAL OF MARITAL
> AND FAMILY THERAPY (2001)

It was 8:20 P.M. It was a Tuesday night. It was a first date. And I was having an absolute panic attack. Actually, I wouldn't have let myself have a full-on attack complete with *tears* because that would have ruined my mascara, but I was at least having trouble breathing

1

and had a slight pain in my chest. The catalyst was this: My date, a cute, young doctor, was 20 minutes late and had not shown yet. I was acting like my father had just died.

While a part of me knew that my knight-in-shining-armor (for the moment) was indeed on his way, another part of me felt utter terror about the possibility of being stood up. Consequently, when the guy finally did show his adorable face at my apartment door, my fear had somehow morphed into anger, and there was not much he could do to win me over. Granted, showing up 20 minutes late on a first date is somewhat rude, a great indicator that a man doesn't respect a woman's boundaries, but my panic at his lateness was way over the top. It was the kind of anger more suited for a late car-service pickup, not a truant boy-toy. Yet my brain had confused the two. Obviously, I had some "issues" I was unaware of. In short, I was lousy girlfriend material.

What Is a Great Girlfriend?

I have a giant confession to make. When I began to write this book, I had no idea about how to truly be great girlfriend material. I mean, I know what fashion magazines tell us about creating physical attractiveness and I can name a few smart girlfriend tricks that seemed to have worked in some of my own relationships, but I never really knew what *great girlfriend material* meant from a man's point of view. For better or worse, I had never been inside the head of a man.

Besides being uninformed on the subject, I was also crippled with prejudice. Forgive my sexist perspective, but since learning that the average man's use of the Internet is limited to the three *S*'s—stocks, sports, and sex—I assumed that those subjects occupied most of the real estate in guys' noggins. Since those three *S*'s loosely translate into "make money, fight, and get laid," I also figured that anything else of value—like, oh ya, *feelings*—was tucked away in some low-rent walk-up in their cerebral cortex to be unearthed only by their mothers. Remember who Puff Daddy, er, I mean P-Diddy, gushed with gratitude for when his butt was saved from jail? That's right. His manly tears spilled for Mom and his almighty. Granted, he couldn't thank his girlfriend who had split during his trial. But I'll bet this wasn't the first time that Mom caused a stir in his, uh, in his *heart*.

Now here's where my confession continues. I'm taking a deep breath now. I was W-R-O-N-G. Men actually have feelings and want more from women than sex. Wow. As I began to interview many men and ask them to confide in me about what worked and what didn't work in women's games of seduction, I was stunned to hear very little about physical attraction, and a whole lot about emotional qualities. When asked what made a woman a great catch, I heard nothing about face makeup and plenty about brain makeup. I was stunned.

Granted, at times, trying to obtain adjectives to explain cliché terms like *needy* and *high maintenance* was like pulling teeth. I stand by my sexist opinion that we women are the gender that excels in language. Men are the gender that excels in keeping secrets. To back me up, psychologists have a diagnosis for people who have an inability to express feelings with words. It's called alexithymia. In fact, the condition is so widespread among American males that a new subgroup has been added to the disorder; it's called normative male alexithymia. Basically, it means "can't find words for feelings." I swear, this is a bona fide psychological diagnosis, the kind that keeps therapists in business. And, it keeps regular women, like me, near insanity.

My Search for Commitment-Minded Men

The first challenge, of course, was finding credible men to speak on the subject of grading and rating women. I interviewed a couple dozen single men, but somehow felt I needed more support for their criticisms because I couldn't be certain that they weren't blaming women for their own dating shortcomings. Think of women who complain that all men are jerks, when they're the ones choosing them and putting up with their bad behavior! Now think of single men who blame their situation on women who they say "play head games," "are gold diggers," or, that statement I had to wince at more than a few times, "are just too emotional." When you hear a single man talk like that, don't you wonder what his failings might be? I, for one, usually congratulate him on devising such an efficient strategy to protect himself from intimacy: A good offense is the best defense. Works on the football field as well as in the game of love.

I had hoped that married men would provide the bulk of my material, but I had another concern there—that they wouldn't even remember the dating scene, or that it had changed a lot since they left it. I know that absence makes the heart grow fonder, but I also know that the absence of an active bachelor life might elicit nostalgic stories that, though wonderful to hear, would probably be far from the truth. I needed men who were familiar with the current dating scene yet definitely commitment minded.

I decided to focus mainly on men who had *recently* made a commitment to a woman. These included newly engaged men, newlywed men, newly cohabiting men, and men who had been upstanding boyfriends of at least six months. (I depended on their girlfriends' nod for proof of their good-boyfriend status.)

So with my target population identified, I ventured forth to get the opinions of this strange species called commitment-minded men.

They were surprisingly easy to find, though harder to get to talk. After exhausting the verbal capacities of the one at home (yes, this extrovert has chosen to live with a quiet introvert), I posted notices on web sites, gabbed with my seatmates in business class, and made a beeline at social gatherings for my girlfriends' newly crowned boyfriends and husbands—with their permission, of course.

In the end, I talked to more than one hundred men. My pool of male experts included members of four ethnic categories and ranged in age from 21 to 50. I padded my research with my currently-dating-men interviews and even sought the advice of matchmakers and relationships coaches who work with men. Finally, I scoured the Internet for the latest scientific studies on dating, mating, and male/female behavior.

I hope all my research captures the voice of the average male, but I must remind you that this is not science. My work as a journalist is largely anecdotal and I am limited by the particular features of my study population. For instance, since I found most of my subjects either through the Internet (bridal sites were particularly helpful) or through referrals from my peer group of young professionals, I don't think I gathered a wide enough economic range. Missing might be those who are unemployed, low-income, or at the other end of the scale, extremely wealthy. Also missing are detailed pictures of cultural courting practices. Not every respondent or interview subject chose to reveal his race to me, so I am unable to make any generalizations about cultural differences.

Almost all of my interviews for this book were conducted through anonymous phone contact, as I wanted men to feel safe being honest. Many of our conversations lasted an hour or more and some even exceeded two hours. I loved it when I got a man who was a talker! A core group of men completed a detailed 50-question survey that I e-mailed to them. Most of the direct quotes you'll read in this book come from those surveys, and the identities of the respondents are concealed to protect them.

I truly thank all the men who helped me with this project. I hope their insights help us test our own aptitude at being better girlfriends or girlfriend material. I, for one, was grateful for the help.

Guess What? I Got Men to Say the "F" Word: Feelings

So, what did I learn? Well, first of all, give me a medal. I attempted to do the impossible: get men to talk about their feelings regarding a woman. And, surprisingly, with some gentle coaxing, I managed to gain insight into men that might be earth shattering to some women. For instance, did you know that when we, out of the goodness of our kind hearts, offer to contribute to that first-date check, most men think we're telling them that we are not attracted to them and won't be sleeping with them in the near or far future? And we just wanted to show them that we are financially independent!

The Role of Boyfriend Is Best Played by a Boy

And, speaking of independent women, I also found men have a hard time when we are too independent. According to men, many women today seem to have confused independence with Nazi-style aggression. As a feminist, I squirmed in my chair through many an interview with a man who described women as being too much like men. Apparently, a byproduct of our economic accomplishments is an inability to turn off our competitive nature when we hit the dinner table. "Too much male energy!" was the reigning complaint of my research.

Because I wanted to be sure that these men weren't pining for an old-fashioned play of female passivity, I really grilled them about what "male energy" meant to them. I heard words like *controlling, competitive, aggressive, angry, pushy,* and *demanding.* Okay, I thought, all those adjectives are part of a description of a normal healthy woman who has obvious unfulfilled needs—I mean, how can you get the care you deserve, whether it be at the hair salon or emergency ward, unless you are sort of demanding about it? And when someone crosses one of our precious boundaries, we have a right to be angry, right?

Well, the problem, according to men, is that we get defensive and controlling *long before* any hurt happens and when we ask for help in a hostile way. Some men even suspected that they were being punished for all the previous bad-boys in women's lives. One guy told me he has to repeat over and over to his girlfriend, "I am not your ex-boyfriend!"

Men told me that, too often, women enter a dating dynamic with a preconceived plan in mind—a sort of Cinderella story— and then try to mold the man to their plan, rather than getting to know them first and then creating a plan together. Ahh, so that's what men call male energy, being an architect or an orchestra leader, rather than a partner. Interesting that men give themselves so much bad press.

In this book, I plan to share all of those insights and tips for better girlfriend behavior. Here is a message from the other half of our species.

It's a Test, But Take It Lightheartedly

Those readers who may have purchased my first book, *The Boyfriend Test,* know that I like to write in a fun, easy-to-digest vernacular with the latest psychological research woven in for substance. And I really enjoy creating tests with score sheets because I think they're fun. I also write many things that are intended as humor. Please remember that all comedy is just tragedy viewed from across the street. And sometimes that street has to be pretty wide for one to see the comedic perspective. It is not my intention to malign women by creating what some might consider to be a silly test that focuses on women's failings. Instead, I am trying to inject some humor into a serious subject—painful heartbreak and the journey toward intimately connecting with another human. So take a break, my girlfriends. Let's laugh at ourselves and our dating errors. As you're about to read, I am guilty of too much of what men have complained about.

why do men commit?

> Grief can take care of itself, but to get the full value of joy you must have somebody to divide it with.
>
> MARK TWAIN, *NOTEBOOK* (1935)

Why do men commit? And who are these guys, anyway? They never seemed to be the ones sliding up beside *me* at the bar.

Well, the simple answer is that men commit for the same reasons women do. It's a basic instinct for humans to want to bond with each other. The urge to commit one's heart, body, and money to another person may be fueled by three compo-nents: Biology, Culture, and Psychology.

The biological pressure to commit is probably the easiest to explain. Men (and women) are wired to reproduce. It's that simple. In some way men are a gazillion sperm in search of an ovum. You don't have to date many heterosexual men to know this is true. But if the only reason men desire to commit is to have sex, we'd see far more lifelong bachelors who would be more clever at obtaining sex. Bad pickup lines would be obsolete.

The next reason why men commit is a social one. We are a culture that preaches long-term monogamy—like a term of half a century. Not that it's happening much in large urban centers, where partner recycling seems to happen every four to seven years, but a forty-year marriage is still a cultural goal, nonetheless. If you stopped one hundred people on the street and told them you had just had your fortieth wedding anniver-sary, you would obtain far more congratulations than condo-lences. This awe of long-term commitment has ancient roots that date back to the beginning of our modern industrial society.

The Evolution of Marriage

To understand how we became a society that reveres long-term monogamy over frequent partner exchanges, you need a little history lesson. And I mean an ancient history lesson. Here goes. First came the dark ages—humans roamed in clans as hunters and gatherers. Think cavemen and cavewomen. Being women, our job was to gather a bounty of yummy fruits, nuts, and veggies. We hooked up with a cute hunter who could bring home great meat. Sometimes we had a baby with him. We kept him during our most vulnerable years—of pregnancy and nursing. He was great protection for us because he was programmed to protect his genes, and, well, his genes were attached to our womb and then our boob—for years. That was before infant formula, Gerber baby food, and food processors. Our breast was the only source of nutrition for infants and toddlers without molars.

Back then we usually dumped our guy when our kid was about three or four because we wanted to go out with the girls again and besides, he started sharing that meat with too many other women anyway. Then we spotted another cute guy. Now he was a really great hunter. And so on. And so on.

Fast forward a few hundred thousand years. Next came farming and agriculture. Our man planted some seeds and stayed in one place to watch them grow. We hung around for the harvest too and, while on the farm, decided to make ourselves useful. We found that we could make a simple hut into a loving home. He liked that. We stayed with him much longer than we had in the past because we were isolated on a plot of land, and meeting a cute hunter was hard to do. We missed the flock of women who helped with the kids but we still got together for weaving groups, quilting bees, and much later, stock market investment clubs. But I'm getting ahead of myself.

Next came industry. Our men hustled off to the mines, the factories, and eventually the office. And they brought home something very unique. Instead of a slain deer, or a bushel of wheat, they came home with a handful of silver coins, or some funny green paper, or a plastic card. All these items held power at the food market. Oh ya, we started going to food markets to get those nuts and things that we used to find all by ourselves. By now we'd forgotten how to be good gatherers. Our grand-mothers stopped telling us which root could be poison back when we lived on farms and grew only the safe kinds. Our men left the farms because they thought it was easier to earn money than sow crops. And where were *we*? In the house, with some children, working hard to make his home a happy one so he would keep us and keep bringing home that green stuff. And I don't mean artichokes. We nicely asked if we could also work in the factories, mines, and offices, but were politely declined. Men were no dummies. They needed someone to stay with their kids. And they needed us to be needy, so we'd stay—and keep our ovum in their house.

According to feminist historians, both the agricultural age and the industrial revolution disempowered women. We were no longer the central hub of the species, parenting in sisterly sororities of aunties, mothers, grannies, and cousins. By the way, did you know that in modern hunter-gatherer societies (there are still a few today) the gatherers produce more calories on a monthly basis than the hunters do? Yes, women were the backbone of the "survival of the fittest" code for millions of years.

However, back in the agricultural age women were not to be undone. After all, we are smart cookies and not about to be victims for long. If we were going to be holed up in his shanty for a lifetime, we wanted a contract. So we organized a union. That union was made up of the church, the government, and a bevy of social pressures. All parties had an interest in keeping us from abandoning the farm and leaving hungry kids for society to deal with. And so our first official employment contract was drawn up. It was called marriage. It was so official we eventually needed a license, blood tests, and even our own attorney. It was financial protection for us, for life. Okay, he got to put in one clause—we had to give up the boots at least once. That's called consummating the union. Thankfully most of us liked giving up the boots (unless they're Manolo Blahniks), so we did it many times over the course of the contract.

And, believe it or not, all that wasn't so long ago. The end result is today's version of marriage. It may or may not involve a church, a courthouse, and a public nod of approval. But, if you don't think that some part of today's man isn't motivated to commit because of societal pressure, you are wrong, girlfriend. Whether it's to please his mom, or marry in a church because his brother did, or buy his girlfriend a diamond so his friends can see how rich he is, most men are under some subtle societal pressure to commit to long-term monogamy.

But not all men. Since the sexual revolution of the 1960s and '70s, plenty of men have been in no hurry to commit to long-term monogamy. Cultural pressure to commit has lessened. And for good reason. In the words of an admonishing fifties-era mother, "Why buy a cow when you can get the milk for free?" Oh ya, I forgot to mention that when we drew up that employment contract, we were supposed to be virgins and withhold any sex until after the contract was signed by both parties. Dating must have been so boring, not to mention frustrating, back then.

So, by owning our own orgasm, did we screw ourselves? (Pun intended.) Not really. Because there is one other powerful and complicated component to commitment—psychology. Okay. Now we can separate the wheat from the chaff and really talk turkey about why some men commit and some don't. In my opinion, in the absence of biological and cultural pressures, the psychological factor reigns supreme.

Why Are There No Grooms Magazines?

It's no secret that men in general have a hard time committing. Few men grow up with the lifelong dream of walking down the aisle with a bride. At 18, they don't fantasize about the perfect tux and the most romantic wedding. Not only are men jittery about the idea of weddings but many are phobic about the whole commitment thing in any form. Many don't really want to be serious boyfriends, either.

There's a little history to commitment phobia, too. Way back when marriage was primarily an economic union, it was a fair exchange. Men had the money. Women had the womb and the housekeeping skills. No matter that many believe it was a kind of prison for women; from a man's perspective, it was also a prison for them—a place where someone *else* spent most of their money. A place where expensive children kept appearing. A place where there was pressure to produce much more than food on the table. After all, we saw a lot of cute material goods at those quilting bees and often came home with, "Honey, the Joneses have a new dishwasher," "second car," "vacation home," etc. We expected him to help us keep up with them. That's a lot of pressure for one guy.

Of course, it's different today with us bringing home a paycheck, too, but not really. It's true that in more than a quarter of American marriages, the woman earns *more* money than her husband and in another quarter, she earns equal money. So, today marriage isn't always an economic trap for men. Except that now we've upped the ante and, because of our paychecks, expect to keep up with not only the Joneses but also the Rockefellers.

And now that we've gained some economic power at home, we women are also putting pressure on men to commit more than resources. A good paycheck isn't enough anymore. We can get that ourselves. We need much more from men today. We want intimacy! We want a satisfying sex life! We want a participatory father! And, yes, we still want the trash carried out! That's why committing to a woman is more scary for men than ever.

Becoming Attached

The thing that will supersede that fear for men is inclination. Psychological makeup is a big factor in ability to commit. It matters not if he wants to commit. Your concern should be, "Is he able to commit?" Commitment-minded men have a specific psychological makeup that's pretty easy to spot once you know what to look for.

We are all hard-wired as babies and children to attach to people in a certain way. In recent years there has been tremendous research on infant psychology and even the impact of womb experiences on personality. Of paramount importance seems to be the bond with mother and infant—whether it happens and how successful it is. Through this research, psychologists have come up with a powerful idea called Attachment Theory.

According to this school of thought, everyone, it seems, has a certain kind of attachment organization based on the kind of parenting they received in the first years of life. By the way, the seeds of Attachment Theory were sowed in the 1940s and '50s when doctors noticed that hospitalized children, isolated from their parents to prevent the spread of germs, stopped crying for their mothers after some time and, indeed, acted indifferent when their parents finally were allowed to visit. Later many of the mothers complained that it was a "different" child who came home from the hospital, a bullying, unkind, or unempathetic individual. Thus began the search for the roots of personality in the mother/child relationship.

The theory is this: If a child's basic emotional and physical needs are met at home, then that person has a good chance of growing up to trust people, to trust love, and to seek out partners who help him re-create that familiar feeling of mother-love. These people have what is referred to as "secure attachment" organization. As adults they bond easily and move away from those who are hurtful. These are true commitment-minded men and women. And I am referring to their deepest subconscious mindedness, not their intellectual brains that on a date brag to you they want to commit.

Other people have more anxiety about attachment. They are "anxiously attached." Perhaps their mom or dad didn't comfort them consistently when they cried. Maybe a parent disappeared for a period during infancy. Maybe there were just too many siblings to share the mommy-love. Maybe his parents were even abusive. For many reasons, anxiously attached people don't trust the feeling of love. It gives them anxiety and a feeling that they don't know what's coming next. Children of alcoholic parents often fall into this category. Their parents gave them one kind of love when sober and another kind when intoxicated. These people are so familiar with the feelings of pain and love mixed together that that's what they seek out! Anxiously attached people can be either clingy, sending potential partners running for cover from endless separation anxiety, thereby reinjuring themselves by feeling abandoned when a partner takes off, or they can alternate between smothering their mates and pushing them away. Finally, they can actually create conflict in a relationship that's running smoothly because conflict is more familiar to them than harmony.

Finally, there are those who cope with feelings of childhood abandonment by simply detaching and refusing to bond with another. These people are called avoidant attachers. A scenario here might be a baby who is left in a room to "cry it out"; after awhile, that baby learns not to cry, for crying does no good to bring comfort. Or a young child whose neediness causes anger in the mother. Researchers who observed mothers and babies interacting in a lab were fascinated to hear mothers of detached infants proudly brag about how "independent" their baby was. Independent, or detached and unable to bond? I'm thinking now of all the independent men I know in their late thirties and forties who have built successful careers and beautiful homes—and who live alone. These men might turn out to be the "confirmed lifelong bachelors." I am curious about their childhood.

Just yesterday I had a conversation with a young man about Attachment Theory. The twenty-seven-year-old magazine editor didn't know that I was interviewing him about attachment, and if he had known, he may have been lost in the theoretical jargon that psychologists delight in hiding behind. No, this man thought I was interviewing him about, of course, dating. And his frank language about such a complex subject confirmed what so many attachment theorists preach—that early bonding experiences are carried forward in life as a kind of blueprint for peer relationships. We seek out partners who fulfill our expecta-tions (positive or negative) and if they don't give us the reac-tions we are familiar with, then we increase behaviors that might elicit the responses we "need."

Back to my young, frustrated single man. He was bemoaning the telephone games that women play with men. "I'm fine with approaching a woman," he said, "I have no problem asking for her number and taking her on a great date. It's the thing that comes after that I hate. Women send mixed messages. They're there. They're not there. I just want them to tell me if they like me or not."

Later in our conversation I asked him about his parents and family upbringing. His response regarding his mother was at first dismissive, saying, "I had a great mom." But later, after describing her ambitious career, he amended his appraisal by adding a small, though telling, caveat, "I had a great mom, when she was there." His tone of voice so mirrored his description of the women he dates that I half expected him to add, "I wish she would just tell me if she likes me or not."

Of course, one anecdotal conversation is hardly grounds for a diagnosis, but the conversation got me thinking about the dozens of other interviews I had done with men, and how they pointed to Attachment Theory. I wondered about the early life experiences of men who described women as "too needy and smothering," or others who seemed to crave an instant fusion and rejected a woman if she didn't have sex with them on the first date. I remember a particularly poignant interview with a man who, in an unemotional monotone, described a mother who "as long as he could remember" was detached and uncaring. This man was thirty-nine years old, an exceptionally wealthy investment banker, and none of his adult romantic relationships had ever exceeded nine months—the length of a pregnancy. Maybe his womb experience was the only healthy attachment he had known.

Attachment Theory holds so many keys to adult romantic pair bonding. The unique mating dance of couples is choreographed by the internal world of both partners, creating, in the end, a performance that runs the gamut from an embracing waltz to one where the dancers continually step on each other's feet. It is a reflection of the secret world of an infant and parent, played out again, with a grown-up body and a new kind of caregiver—a lover.

Long-term studies have illuminated this mystery and put theory into the hands of calculable science. Adolescents have actually been tested, through questionnaires and observations of them hanging out with their parents, and then been categorized as either secure, anxious, or detached. Years later, researchers tested those same adolescents, who had become young adults, and this time looked at their style of attachment with their romantic partner. Sure enough, the adult relationship mirrored the parent-child relationship.

But all this research supporting the strong ties between parenting and pair bonding is not a death sentence for love. Insecure attachment organization is not irreversible. The healing power of a therapeutic alliance, yep, I mean you and a trusted therapist alone in an office, can go a long way to repairing the damage done at home.

True, we all have different relationship styles. And the way we attach to another is an unconscious process. We're usually not aware of what we're doing and our really clever brains come up with all kinds of excuses for our singlehood. The answer, of course, is to probe our unconscious self and slowly learn to separate the past from the present. Psychologists call this a transformation of an internal working model. I call it the shift in our perspective that lets us see how much control we really have over our love choices and relationship behaviors.

He's the Hook, but You're the Fish

Now wouldn't life be easy if the only trick to hooking up were to spot the man with secure attachment style and parade your pretty self in front of him until he, well, until he securely attached? Unfortunately, life is a little more complex. First of all, you've got to be physically attracted to him (and vice versa). I promise you, there are battalions of men with secure attachment organization marching by you every day and you don't care a whiff for their pheromones. And not only do you have to find a secure attacher who is a babe in your eyes, but he also has to be socially acceptable in your world. Whether it's age, religion, politics, lifestyle, whatever, there are a litany of things that might strike this cutie off your list.

Finally—and this is probably the most important part of the equation—you've got to be hookable. You've got to have fairly secure attachment organization yourself. Now don't freak out if you nodded in recognition when you read the descriptions of the insecure attachment styles. Just knowing yourself is the first step to healing. Be equally concerned if you just automatically assumed that you have secure attachment organization. Some researchers suspect that as little as 50 percent of the population are secure in the way they bond. Our anxiety over separation, abandonment, and indeed, intimacy, mostly relates to the parenting styles of our generation.

And it can be overcome. That's the good news. The not-so-good news is that it takes time. It takes practice. It takes honest soul-searching and often professional therapy. Why do you think the divorce rate and the popularity of therapy exploded at the same time for the baby boom generation? Too many babies spaced narrowly together is a prescription for insufficient maternal nurturing—and insecure attachment. Now, in our adult life, we are trying to figure all this out. And we can.

The other bit of good news, ladies, is that our healthy romantic pursuits don't have to be limited to the small group of men who know intuitively how to attach successfully. Gosh, if you narrowed that group even further by excluding men who happen to be uncute in your books and men who were unappealing in other ways, you might be looking for a needle in a haystack. Instead all you have to look for is a man who's aware, or open to becoming aware (as you are, my dear). That doesn't mean we should go around diagnosing our date. It just means gently helping him become aware of the impact of his behavior on you. And it means being honest with yourself while trying to change your ways to accommodate his feelings.

You've got to ask yourself if you're a bit commitment-phobic, too. Do you put men into endless games of telephone tag? Are you forever playing hard to get? Maybe you're not playing. Maybe you *are* hard to get. You've got to understand your own attachment style and to be aware of how it could be sabotaging relationships before they even begin.

For instance, back in my dating days, I was such a bad-boy chaser that I used to dump men if they were too nice. Nice! I was rejecting "Nice" and welcoming "Cruel"! In truth, it was my way of protecting myself from the scary world of intimacy.

Since I didn't trust love, I simply chose untrustworthy men to confirm my beliefs.

The trick to getting conscious about this is to look for patterns in our choices. Have all your partners behaved the same way? For instance, I used to believe that all men were jerks—until I learned that all men are not jerks, only the ones I was choosing. Finding your own role in playing with commitment-phobics is the first step to getting them out of your life and having a healthy relationship. *The Girlfriend Test* will help you do that. It will help you assess your attachment style and help you become aware of your own patterns in relationships. And it will help you make better choices.

Spotting a Commitment-Phobe

A re there any specific things that commitment-phobic men do? There sure are. And you can read all about them in *The Boyfriend Test*. They love the chase. They may be psychologically afraid to commit but they are biologically wired to reproduce. They often rush the sexual aspect of a relationship. And once the sex happens—which is actually a terrifying event for them because it is a form of intimacy—they run. They hide behind answering machines. They take longer and longer to return our calls. And they always have plenty of really good excuses for their behavior. They tell us they still like us, but at the same time they move away from us. It can be a very confusing message.

One man I interviewed was delightfully candid about this subject. He was a CIT, a commitment-phobe in transition, and his newfound awareness was refreshing. He told me he actually was one of those players who loved to hit and run, though he didn't always like himself afterward. He said he bought into the sexualized message of our culture—that more partners mean better sex—and, at 19, took that message to a college out of state. This young, and very attractive, young man claims that during his four-year B.A., where he majored in English, he also got a minor in sexual education, bedding every attractive woman on the entire campus in a personal game of conquest.

But this particular player had a conscience, and felt bad about hurting so many women. Thus his eventual journey through therapy and his ability, at the age of 28, to talk to me so openly about his feelings. Our conversation started in a coffee shop and ended up in a parking garage, and his greatest moment came just before he disappeared down the dark corridor to his parked car: "Please tell women," he whispered, "when they meet men like me, to please slow me down. Just slow us down. Don't have sex with me on the first date. It's too much. I'll just run away."

Just like the man said, there is only one way to protect your heart from a commitment-phobe. I'll be talking more about this in chapter 8, "The Girlfriend Sex Test." Slow down the sexual pace of a relationship and try to build emotional intimacy instead. And explain it to him as you're doing it. I promise you, he is far more frightened of emotional intimacy and will freak out and leave before your heart and body get committed. And, one final word: A commitment-phobic will put a full-court-press on you to obtain sex just before he makes his exit. It's often the only tool he has to try to connect with a woman. Then he'll use that as an excuse to leave. But don't buy into his rationalizations. Don't feel abandoned. Don't feel you did the wrong thing. You won. You protected yourself from a lot of heartache.

And if you do have sex and he runs away, please don't blame yourself. Don't take it personally. His retreat had nothing to do with you.

Spotting a Commitment-Minded Man

There's a handy reference tool that I came up with while researching this book to help me quickly assess a man's commitment potential. I simply look at the three categories of motivators—Biology, Culture, and Psychology—and I try to find at least one item in each category. Take a look at the chart below. If you can get some basic information on the first couple of dates and find that you've got a checkmark in each column, then it is probably safe to proceed with this man.

Biology

1. He's straight.

2. He's not a smooth pickup artist (i.e., probably needs a girlfriend if he wants consistent sex).

3. He tells you he's never had a one-night stand.

4. He likes kids and says he wants to be a father someday.

Culture

1. He's a devout follower of any religion. (Most religions encourage monogamy.)

2. His siblings are married or engaged.

3. He has lots of married friends.

4. He seems to have a plan for his home life. He's thought about where he wants to live, how many kids he'd like to have, and what qualities in a mate (besides beauty!) he's looking for.

Psychology

1. He's available—for phone calls and dates. No hiding. No playing hard to get.

2. He's emotionally available. He's able to use the "F" word, Feelings.

3. He's as concerned about your needs as his. He understands that you may want to slow the sexual pace in order to build intimacy.

4. He's had at least one long-term relationship (three or four years) in his past.

the many faces of eve

A woman can be anything that the man who loves her wants her to be.

J. M. BARRIE, *TOMMY AND GRIZEL* (1900)

The Girlfriend Test is an exercise designed to do two things: (a) figure out who we are, and (b) help us make a healthy connection.

Of those goals, I have to say that figuring out who we are as individuals is the most important, both to having a healthy relationship and to finding happiness in general. The number one complaint that men had about women during my research was that their dates were not being "themselves." Most men, it seems, can see through even our best performances.

But who are we really? And how do we discover her? After all, we gals are under such cultural pressure to conform to some definition of the ideal woman that the danger of digging deep and finding someone who may not be a *Glamour* magazine icon is terrifying. Instead, most of us spend the bulk of our lives costuming ourselves and playing roles that are acceptable in our social circle though incongruent with our true selves. The downside, of course, is that when we wear the masks our culture has painted for us, we'll meet only men who are trapped in their own masks, because like attracts like. Sincere men run away, and no one can have an authentic conversation.

The Masks We Wear

Remember the Jim Carrey movie called *The Mask*? It was a comic look at this same principle. Jim played an insecure guy with no social skills—until he found an ancient tribal mask and became the wild man with the green face and the *über* confidence. Coincidentally, that film comes to mind as I write this because I played a very small role in it. I played a talk show host who was interviewing a psychologist, played by Ben Stein. Stein's character had written a book called *The Masks We Wear* and after seeing our show, Jim's character decides to try on his infamous mask. How ironic that a decade later, I am writing a book that suggests we remove the masks we wear.

But what are these masks and why do we wear them? Well, the important thing to know is that every character we play has a function in our lives. As young children with vulnerable hearts, we start to learn to create a "public face" that helps us negotiate the hurtful world. Even if the mask is an innocent one that uses good manners instead of preschooler aggression, it is just the beginning of burying our true feelings. When we become adults, we've worn our masks for so many years that we have long ago forgotten which feeling it was concealing. We become trapped in our mask, even when it becomes outdated.

Now, I'm not suggesting that wearing a socially acceptable mask as an adult is always a problem. I mean, it's not always functional to tell your boss what you *really* think of her. But there are two caveats to using a social mask in a healthy way: (a) we must constantly remind ourselves that it is just an act and not our true self, and (b) we must remember to take off our mask for our closest intimates.

I think that happens with healthy people. But for the rest of us (like 80 percent of the population!) our masks have been so socially reinforced that we start to believe our own schtick. In Hollywood, when an actor is stuck in his own self-admiration we say that he/she believes their own press. And, in some way, we all believe at least a bit of our own press.

It is understandable. Our parents might not have given us a safe environment to express sadness, anger, fear, guilt, pride, or embarrassment and instead responded with judgment, anxiety, or compulsive helpfulness. As a result we may not even have learned to tolerate our own feelings and instead shoved those feelings into some recess in our brains, ignored but not forgotten. Eventually we created a mask whose main purpose was to comply with others—a compliant face that makes us very likable. Likable, maybe even popular, but not sincere. Unfortunately, those ancient feelings of discontent have a sneaky way of surfacing at the wrong time in the wrong way. Sarcasm, passive-aggressive behaviors, like acting flaky to those whom we love, are ways that those feelings resurface—except now they're likely not under our control but have taken on a damaging life of their own.

Fast-forward twenty years, and we're doing an Academy Award–worthy performance on a date and our guy comes away feeling he's been played. For good reason. He has been played. And at the same time we come away from the date wondering why he didn't like us. After all, we had spent two decades working on that part and rehearsing it for thousands of people!

I know that frustration. I have had that feeling many times. I still have it from time to time because even my mask is not completely torn away. And every once in a while, someone reveals something to me that I may be in denial about. The difference between now and the distant past is that I have the confidence to accept criticism and not go deeper into denial mode. (Most of the time.) Taking off our masks is a lifelong process.

So Who Are We, Anyway?

As women in our American culture, our masks come in a variety of styles. We can be Barbie Dolls, Daddy's Girls, Trophy Wives, Caregivers, and Bad Girls. We can be Material Girls, Workout Queens, Socialites, Professionals, and Hard-Core Mothers.

Granted, all of the roles I've listed may be small parts of who we really are, but none of them completely explains our internal self. Look at that list closely. Every title is geared to please someone else. Whether the object of our role-playing is a man, a child, a boss, our doctor, or a girlfriend, none of the above labels answers to our own inner voice that begs to be paid attention to. Where are the parts of us that are called Artist, Lover, Dreamer, Thinker, or Creator? Well, I promise, if you haven't found those parts of yourself, you're not bringing enough to any relationship table, for it is that intangible thing that some call a soul, that great men really fall for.

Heck, even men whom many would call heartless sex hounds fall in love with the whole woman, not her vagina. One of the men whom I interviewed, a 42-year-old married man with a young child, practically salivated while retelling stories of sexual bravado from his single days. He clearly did not equate sex with intimacy and told me so. In fact, he slept with his now-wife on the second date. Yet, when I asked him what he loves about his wife the most, he told me it was her attachment to the earth. The pleasure she gets from gardening. The look on her face when she received a set of seedlings as a gift from him. The sex-hound playboy smitten with an earth mom? I suspect he was in love not with the label of earth mom but with the authenticity of her feelings and the sincere pleasure she gets in her garden. So, if we never make the time to discover our own needs and experience sheer joy in ourselves, how can we share it with someone?

To illustrate my point, take a look at the roles I played last Tuesday:

TIME	ROLE	ACTIVITY
8:00 A.M.	Mother	Lunch making, teeth brushing, car pooling
9:00 A.M.	Workout Queen	A trip to the gym
10:00 A.M.	Caregiver	Grocery store and dry cleaners
11:00 A.M.	Mother again	Story-time parent at my daughter's school
12:00 P.M.	Barbie Doll	Showering, primping, painting my face for work
1:00 P.M.	Material Girl	Driving my fancy car to work while wearing D&G
2:00 P.M.	Professional	Working on a TV show
7:00 P.M.	Trophy Wife	Hosting a dinner for family and friends

Looking at this list, I have to ask myself, "Where was Wendy?" Oh sure, you could argue that the trip to the gym was a sweet indulgence and Wendy got to benefit from an endorphin high. Or I can tell you that I was there on my doctor's orders because of high cholesterol. You could extol the creative virtues of my Martha-wanna-be dinner party. Or I could be honest and say I was so pressed for time that it was frozen pizza for the kids and takeout for the adults. No, this day was not exactly personally gratifying.

Now, let's imagine, in a perfect fantasy world, that I could erase all those role-playing women and replace them with just Wendy. Wendy alone on an island just being. Hey, while you're reading this, why don't you insert your own name into this fantasy? Let's make this dream a party. So, there you are, alone on an island, Karen, Jody, Maria, Sandy, Dawn, Carrie, or whoever, and you open your eyes to a bright light. It's morning. The sun is just rising above the ocean. And the first thing you say to yourself is, "Today I'm going to . . . "

And your answer is? Well, I know for sure that driving on a freeway with Victoria's Secret irritating my tender parts is definitely *not* going to be on my to-do list that day. Ditto on the errand running. No dry cleaners on my island. What did you answer?

My psyche answered: Arrange some flowers, read an anthropology book, jog on the beach, sit and think, and then write at your computer. (It may be an island, but mine has amenities.)

So what does this fantasy day have to do with passing The Girlfriend Test? Well, if I had happened to go on a date after that busy Tuesday, my lively social chitchat would be most intriguing to a would-be suitor if it included which of the following:

> **A.** the chaos of car pool
> **B.** my battle with my G-string
> **C.** the trouble with dry cleaners
> **D.** an interesting thought that I had that day.

I'm placing my bet on answer D. Finding things inside yourself and sharing them with another is very alluring. Unless, of course, the first thing you find inside yourself is repressed anger. Leave that off a first-date subject list and take it straight to an empathetic therapist.

I found one of the most extreme examples of a woman who hadn't found herself in the Hollywood movie *The Runaway Bride*. Julia Roberts literally ran from the altar four times, not because she was afraid of commitment, but because deep down, she knew that her grooms loved not her but the girl who answered to their needs so well. She had unconsciously mirrored those suitors so perfectly—right down to sharing their tastes for food—that without a man she wasn't even sure how she liked her own eggs cooked! In the end of the movie, however, she gets down on one knee and proposes to Richard Gere—but only *after* she starts a small business selling her own designer lamps and develops a love for eggs Benedict.

The Faces We Wear

While quizzing my committed men, I heard all kinds of slang labels for women who aren't being entirely themselves. She's a "Miss Priss," "a Glamour Puss," "a Jock," "a Control Freak." I asked the men who used these terms for further explanations and got a peek into how men perceive us. I decided to spend some time thinking about these characters that we play so well. I wanted to know why we play them and what message we think we're sending out when we play these roles.

Men love to categorize women into certain "types." It helps them remember us. When we're referred to as the blonde, or the six-footer, or the doctor, or the divorcée I'm dating, we can be forgiving because that's just a simple schematic way for them to put order in their harem, er, I mean world. But when negative personality traits become our defining labels, then we should worry a bit. The truth is that all of us can represent all those people, not in a Sybil sort of way, but in a well-balanced personality kind of way. However, if you look closely at yourself, you may find that one stereotype has become your dominant personality and there is little room for the rest of your feminine persona. So read the following definitions carefully and see if any describe you a little too much.

The Daddy's Girl

The Daddy's Girl is so classic, she's become a cliché. And she comes in two types. Type A is not looking for a partner, but for a man her family will approve of. If she's got a dominant father who has a position for him in his firm, her mission is all business. Type B has a Daddy complex because she never fully separated from him. No man will be as good as her father was/is. Note: Type B sometimes even dates men of her father's generation.

I once knew a 35-year-old single woman who wore her long blond hair with bangs and wore flitty skirts that reminded me of a cheerleader. She dated lovely older men and talked in a soft little-girl voice complete with giggles every time a man spoke. Her father had gotten her a job as a sales rep at his company, but when his bosses finally got tired of a sales rep who wasn't selling much, she lost her job. Instead of looking for a new job, sweet Daddy-to-the-rescue suggested she leave her apartment and move back in with him and Mom. Despite the flurry of men she had recently been dating, on moving day a truck showed up with one mover—her father.

Why It Pays to Be a Daddy's Girl: This is an easy one. The Daddy's Girl always has her knight-in-shining-armor. She has no worry about individuating, no worries about being truly independent, and no need to even think about her own needs. Her family has defined her future boyfriend for her—if they let her have one at all.

The Downside of Being a Daddy's Girl: Dads often exact an emotional wage on their adult daughters for decades after it's legal. Potential boyfriends run from entering an older/younger competition, unless they'd really love to work for their father-in-law, and then you have to question their love for you. Sometimes Daddies die, often before another prince charming shows up.

The Barbie Doll

I know this chick well because she dominated my persona for years. This woman ingests the message of our advertising community that being thin, rich, and beautiful is the route to happiness. Barbie is always impeccably dressed and looks so pulled together you can barely see the cracks in her psyche. Men love this woman because she's so well packaged. Her sexual power is enormous. Her economic power is a goal that she may have attained already. *Vogue* magazine is her bible and men are her sheep.

Think of Reese Witherspoon in the movie *Legally Blonde*. She's the "perfect" woman.

Why It Pays to Be a Barbie Doll: Let's face it. Barbie
is the most culturally accepted female role model around. She can win many contests and catch many men.

The Downside of Being a Barbie Doll: Barbie is
a narrow definition of woman. She's not creative. She's not athletic. She's not supposed to be aggressive. And she's certainly never allowed to be sad and vulnerable. Part of Barbie's allure is that she is an advertisement for happiness. In a word, Barbie isn't a real human and when we become Barbies, we have to put an enormous amount of energy into denying and suppressing a great part of ourselves.

The Jockette

I gotta admit, I deeply admire this woman. She's got equality with the boys' club and she knows how to play their game—literally. The Jockette spends more time in Nikes than heels and prides herself on the fact that she has transcended our culture's narrow definition of the female gender. She is strong. She is competitive. She probably shoots hoops with the guys on the weekends. She is well liked by women because she is strong and independent, and respected by men for her athletic skills.

Why It Pays to Be a Jockette: My favorite Nike T-shirt
reads "Women Have Many Needs." The payoff line on the back

of the shirt reads "To Run, Kick, and to Score." And that's how I feel about Miss Jockette. She's able to act out our competitive and aggressive sides in a healthy way. She learned the great messages about teamwork, practice, and competition, things she can even apply to the business world.

The Downside of Being a Jockette: Again, this is a one-note woman who may feel insecure in traditionally feminine roles. Case in point: Check out Sanaa Lathan's character in the movie *Love and Basketball.* This character developed one aspect of herself to the exclusion of the others. Men may have trouble responding to so much masculine energy that's not tempered with some feminine softness.

The Girl's Girl

The Girl's Girl is the estrogen buddy we all love to hang with. She's a hardcore member of the girls' club and is there for us in times of need—especially when we've checked into Heartbreak Hotel. She's great at chick flicks, gets us involved in all kinds of worthy charities and women's business networking organizations, and even helps us entertain when we're throwing a party. Actually, the girl's girl is usually the one who throws *us* a birthday bash. In short, we *love* her.

Why It Pays to Be a Girl's Girl: The Girl's Girl has created a built-in support system for herself. She's so giving and loving to her friends that she knows they'll be there for her when she's in need. She's also created a kind of intimacy with her girlfriends that may satisfy her emotional needs. She's well rounded, "happy," and rarely alone.

The Downside of Being a Girl's Girl: Let's face it, those lucky friends of hers may actually be a surrogate for a male-female relationship. In some ways those friendships may even protect her from intimacy with a man, something she might crave and also fear. And, men may be scared off by dating her *and* all her friends. Finally, her gal pals might all bed down with a hunk in the same year and Miss Girl's Girl may find herself abandoned.

The Material Girl

Madonna sang about her in the 1980s, "We are living in a material world / And I am a material girl." At least Miss Blonde Ambition admitted it. The rest of the pack, I think, subconsciously aspires to wealth. The Material Girl dreams about big houses, salivates over Martha Stewart's entertaining ideas, and pays too much attention to the "Wedding" section of *Town & Country* magazine. This woman knows every brand of luxury watch, car, and designer label, even if she can't afford a piece of it. And Material Girls who are good at what they do always get what they want.

Why It Pays to Be a Material Girl: This woman is a survivor. She has figured out early on that her skills are best applied to resource extraction from a man (even if she has her own job) and she aims high and mighty in her material pursuits. The best part is that if she gets a fair prenup, she'll be financially secure forever.

The Downside of Being a Material Girl: Putting one goal above all others can be limiting. The Material Girl yearns for a rich man but there are no guarantees that he will also be smart, nice, kind, or empathetic. In fact the likelihood is great that he's bought into the same cultural ad campaign as she and hopes to exchange for his money a woman with eternal youth and sex appeal—and that's a lifelong pressure for our Material Girl. Unless, of course, he trades her in for a newer model when she gets old. Finally, the payoff on that prenup might look good at today's interest rates, but factor in inflation, a bad economy, a dip in the stock market, and a tough matrimony lawyer, and our Material Girl might just end up broke and alone. Ouch!

The Miss Priss

This woman is a rule follower and a slave to social convention. Miss Priss has perfect etiquette, perfect manners, and radar for men who want to follow her up the social and/or business ladder. She may be a product of an East Coast prep school. She knows right from wrong and believes she's always right. She's also well liked, has a "safe" circle of friends, is adoring to her family, and lives in a well-groomed community. Miss Priss also hates camping unless J.Crew outfits her for the trip. Her family probably votes Republican.

Why It Pays to Be a Miss Priss: This woman knows what to expect in life. Not too many unexpected sticky situations are coming her way. There are certain unspoken rules that everyone follows, and that's reassuring to her. Within her world, Miss Priss has tons of self-confidence.

The Downside of Being a Miss Priss: This woman may be a big fish in a small pond, but the world is an ocean. She's missing millions of exotic fish who may be swimming all around her. Miss Priss is limited in how much she can grow because she shuts herself off from free-thinking, culturally diverse, politically inspired men. This woman might fall apart if she were ever invited to jump on the back of a Harley with a tattoo-sporting peace activist who hang glides on weekends. Welcome to the real world, Miss Priss.

The Corporate Cat

I once sat beside this woman on a bicoastal plane ride. She embodied the full stereotype of the Corporate Cat. Navy pant suit (silk scarf at neck). Expensive briefcase. Hair clipped back in a chignon. Very little makeup. No jewelry beyond the requisite small gold earrings. Oh, and she told me she had been made a vice president in her company. I spent five hours grilling this woman about her life. She's forty, single, childless, has many male friends. She's usually the only woman in her group at high-end business conferences. She says she works hard to be accepted by the boys' club, being careful to conceal her sexuality, never wearing form-fitting clothes or much makeup, or even letting down her hair. She sees all those feminine trappings as signs of weakness at her level of corporate America—she would never want to be accused of "using" her femininity at the office. She feels proud that she has been completely accepted into the boys' club, on their terms.

Why It Pays to Be a Corporate Cat: Money, prestige, a corner office with a window, a high-rise condo, and equity with the boys' club. How cool. This woman also told me she feels privileged that, because of her position of power, she can create many business opportunities for women. How rewarding. Of course, after a couple of drinks, she admitted to me that the main reason she hires lots of women, especially single mothers, is that they work harder and cost less than men.

The Downside of Being a Corporate Cat: Again, this is a one-note woman who hasn't developed herself as a multifaceted woman. She needs to get in touch with her sexuality, her feminine energy, and the girls' club to really be whole. Note that although she has many male friends and associates, she lives alone. And finally, it's not helping women much to behave exactly like a man in the workplace. Feminine powers of intuition and empathy make for good managers.

The Chatty Cathy

Women excel at language. This woman has taken her verbal skills to the max. She loves to chat on the phone, via e-mail, in the bank line, and to her guy. She is Miss Friendly and can fill any uncomfortable silence with a smile and some lively banter. And she's filled with lots of anecdotal, useful, and entertaining information.

Why It Pays to Be a Chatty Cathy: Some men love this chatter who can fill in the blanks for them. Everyone loves an entertaining gossip. And Cathy can cover her own feelings of nervousness with words, words, words. She might even profit from her gift by becoming a news reporter or writer. Sound like anyone you know? (I wear this mask, too!)

The Downside of Being a Chatty Cathy: Wisdom often shows up in life's silences. Cathy knows none of those. She is far too busy filling in the silence with nervous chatter. And those strong, silent men who love her? They're mostly emotionally repressed men who not only let her do the talking but also the feeling for them. Cathy needs to shut up, meditate, and listen to her inner voice.

The Mirror

This is one of the most common motifs in the masks women wear. As young girls we are taught to cooperate, and that efficient cooperation often incarnates into full-blown mirroring. There's no conflict in our relationships if we simply become "Yes" women. The Mirror knows how to make a man happy. Early on in a relationship she senses what a man wants in a woman and she literally becomes his dream girl, sometimes going as far as to alter her appearance, her career path, or even her values.

Why It Pays to Be a Mirror: Women who are Mirrors for men are rarely without a boyfriend or husband. They are the ultimate in cooperative women. Some men call them easygoing. Others call them perfect.

The Downside of Being a Mirror: Like *The Runaway Bride* illustrates, women who are Mirrors can never truly be happy because their own needs are not being met. Heck, their own needs are not even identified. Women who are Mirrors are so lost in pleasing others (to gain acceptance) that they forget to please themselves.

Who Are You?

I've asked you to look at just a few of the many personas that we women wear. Most of us are intricate combinations of a few of these and none of them are all wrong. As I've illustrated, there is a dose of functionality in every role we play. Problems arise only when the role plays us and we literally forget who we are.

I'm a big fan of meditation as a remedy for the disease of lost self. There are plenty of great books out there on the art of meditation—a couple are included in my bibliography—so I won't try to teach you about that here. But I do suggest that you take thirty minutes a day to just slow down and feel. Sit, lie, or walk slowly, if you must, but just stop thinking! Start breathing and feeling. You might be surprised by the gush of tears or the rush of emotions, even anger. But you must get in touch with yourself. She's a beautiful person and the world is awaiting her arrival.

are you good girlfriend material?

Intimacy begins with oneself.
It does no good to try to find
intimacy with friends, lovers
and family if you are starting
out from alienation and division
within yourself.

THOMAS MOORE, *SOULMATES* (1994)

With this chapter comes the beginning of the test, although this particular part of the test isn't scored. This is an opportunity to internally reflect on who we tend to be in terms of relationships—an opportunity to really answer the philosophical question of "Are we good girlfriend material?"

This is also a chapter full of personal confessions. As I write this I feel like I'm standing on stage at an AA meeting filled with supportive girls' club members. I adjust the microphone. It bleeps with the piercing pitch of audio feedback while I stand nervously looking at the crowd. I carefully step up to the mike, clear my throat, pause, and then finally blurt out, "Oh alright. I admit it. My name is Wendy and I'm a lousy girlfriend."

Well, at least I used to be. That's according to some of my ex-boyfriends whom I've tracked down. You didn't think that I would limit my research to only *your* ex-boyfriends and husbands, did you? No, my dear girlfriends, I did the really brave thing and contacted some of my exes to ask them for postmortem reviews. Humbling was the experience, I'd say. But also in some ways gratifying, for I had wondered what had gone wrong with some of those relationships. Anyway, there was enough material there to add to the insights of the many other men I had interviewed and to write an entire test on the making of a good girlfriend. So, here goes:

Do you like being alone?
I mean, really, really like it?

Do you pride yourself on the fact that, except for procreation, you don't need a man? Are you financially independent? Are you emotionally independent? Do you like the fact that you are not a needy woman? Is your idea of a perfect night a bath, a book, and a little pen dribble in your journal? When you do have him over, are you a little relieved that he's chosen not to stay until breakfast? Okay, girlfriend, here comes your wake-up call.

Have you ever considered that you (we) have become all those things to protect yourself from the terror of intimacy? I hate to break it to you in this way, but there is no greater power than to be vulnerable and, yes, needy in the presence of a man. I know, this sounds counterintuitive, but it is the road to true intimacy.

I remember walking down Fifth Avenue in New York one spring day with a young, attractive male television colleague. It was a chance get-together because he is based in San Francisco and I in L.A. As we walked, the conversation turned to relationships because, when men and women get out of the office, that's usually what they talk about. I had always prided myself on the fact that I did not "need" a man. Sure, I always "wanted" a boyfriend, but I loved to show them all how independent I was. In fact, I was so independent that I even had a bunch of men on my payroll. I had a mechanic. I had a handyman. I had an accountant. I had an attorney and I had a stockbroker—all male. Heck, I even had a male doctor. I thought my dates appreciated the fact that I didn't come whining to them every time my car broke down, or a mutual fund bottomed out, or a pipe leaked at home. Wrong again, Wendy. My young, cute, astute colleague put it in great perspective that spring day in New York. He made the most enlightening statement about me that I could have ever wished for.

"Wendy," he said, "women like you make men feel like we're not needed at all. You make us feel obsolete."

I was stunned. My goal, to be an easygoing, low-maintenance broad, had somehow backfired. I wasn't seen as independent. I was seen as autocratic, insulated, in no need of help, an Ice Queen. Think Sharon Stone in *Basic Instinct*. Think Demi Moore in *Disclosure*. Or, maybe I was seen as simply perfect. Remember, I had perfected a great performance. Yuck! Who wants to spend time with someone so perfect that they make our own foibles glaringly obvious?

About a year after that New York walk, I heard one of my graduate school psychology professors recite this eye-opening definition of intimacy: "The work of intimacy is not only tolerating seeing imperfections in others, but also tolerating the fact that people can now see imperfections in you."

In short, I had to find ways to recognize my needs and humbly make them known to an opposite-gender person. I had to learn how to become healthfully honest about my shortcomings. Scary stuff, that you'll read more about throughout this book.

Do you hate being alone?
Medicating loneliness is not a
reason to seek a boyfriend.

Here's the other side of the same coin—a woman with many
friends who isn't intimate with anyone. Me again. I once had a
birthday party and invited 85 people. When it came time to
blow out the candles, I thanked the crowd for their support and
love during the previous and traumatic two years. I later learned
that one "close" friend of mine whispered to another, "What's
Wendy talking about?" And the response was "Oh, both her
parents died and she took it personally."

A funny line, to be sure, but a great indicator of the level of
intimacy I had with my friends.

So are you the high-energy social creature who can whip up
a crowd of faces at the first threat of a down mood? Is your
speed dial programmed with a full list of "close" friends? When
you find yourself at home alone, do you feel you're missing out
on some "happening" out there? Do you have the television on
even when you're not watching it?

Don't worry, if you answered yes to most of these questions,
you're not completely dysfunctional. I think we place an
unnatural emphasis on independence in America. Why do you
think we have so many problems with intimate relationships?
Because we were given all the tools for independence and few
tools to build healthy *inter*dependence, something that Asian
and Hispanic cultures, for instance, teach a little better. A baby
born in Japan, for instance, is thought to be a separate self that

must be brought into the family ways. Many Americans, on the other hand, think of a newborn as being completely attached— and the parenting emphasis is on promoting separation and independence.

Having said all that, I'm about to do my usual about-face. There is no better way to have a healthy relationship than to learn to be alone in a positive way. What I mean is that being alone is your opportunity to get in touch with your feelings and your needs. It's a chance to get to know yourself free from the external influence of another person's wants and peer pressure. Alone time is also a place to abate ancient feelings of abandonment and separation anxiety—a place to tolerate that discomfort until you can recognize that it is not the least bit about the latest guy who didn't call.

Being alone can be liberating for some women. From your cocoon of alone time you can eventually venture out and develop a few deep, committed relationships.

QUESTION #3

Do you run from conflict?
The urge to take flight when the going gets tough is a behavior not limited to men.

Yes, me—ahem—again. I was once afraid that anger was lethal. I had grown up in a repressed, Catholic, do-gooder household where an angry voice was rarely raised. If I expressed anger at all, I was sent to my room and told to come out when I was happy. The message there: Your anger is not welcome in the world. It is something to be ashamed of. Only cheerful girls are rewarded.

So what did I do when I felt anger in relationships? I ran to my room. Literally. Or, I let it out in an uncontrolled way, because I had bottled it up so much that when it oozed out onto one of my boyfriends, it was nasty. Since I had not learned to fight well, I had also not learned any tools for relationship repair. I thought if anger showed up, then the relationship must be over. So I ran after every fight.

The truth, of course, is that conflict is not the barometer of a healthy relationship. Conflict happens. It should happen. It's part of growing intimate. Relationship health should not be judged on whether conflict happens but on how reparations are made. That's the real work of intimacy. That's how to create trust. So many of the men I interviewed in my research told me that they never knew for sure what women were feeling and when women were angry we really weren't fair fighters, often resorting to sly manipulations or that old-fashioned trick of "I'll make him jealous so he'll want me." Not a good idea. Learn to fight well and you'll learn to love well.

Are you aware of your own feelings?

If you don't learn to pay attention to your feelings, they will amplify themselves and blast out of you in surprising ways.

Do you wonder why you treated that nice guy so badly by being late all the time? What about that Freudian slip when you called him by your ex-boyfriend's name? Do you say things that you regret when you've had a little too much to drink? Do you spend more time being "cool" with guys than being honest?

You could be unaware of your own feelings. Maybe you don't even allow yourself the luxury of psychic suffering. Do you feel abandoned sometimes? Do you feel betrayed? Do you feel rejected? Do you feel that you are not heard? Do you feel that you are being treated mostly as a sex object? Do you feel that your boundaries are being crossed? Do you feel pressure to do things his way? Do you feel scared? Do you *feel* anything?

Congratulations if all these feelings are fresh in your mind and you've sobbed into your pillow, or better yet, in a therapist's office when you've felt this way. For the rest of us, however, these feelings of inadequacy are so painful and repulsive that when the first inkling of rejection creeps into our noggins, we go into great states of denial. We shop. We drink. We exercise. We socialize. We sympathize. We philosophize. We agonize. We analyze. We think and think and think and think and think. But we do not feel. We do not stop and be still and let the pain flow. We don't try to get to the bottom of our issues; instead we build mountains of lies on top of our feelings—which only makes the whole cycle worse, and more mysterious the next time it happens.

Case in point. In *The Boyfriend Test,* I wrote about a particularly painful event when a man whom I really cared about stood me up for Midnight Mass one Christmas Eve. In my first book, I had great fun beating myself up for my poor judgment of his character. Now, to illustrate this point, I want to jump ahead a few years to a time of reconciliation.

Yes, the Christmas Eve guy and I got together again a few years later and had some weeks of intimate, honest conversations and I felt some wonderful feelings of closure on my anger. And, I was pleased to discover that my attraction for him had not waned. It was great. Until one day when he forgot to charge his cell-phone battery and was out of contact. So I morphed this innocent act into a passive-aggressive retreat from me. Granted, the guy had even tried to call me twice that day—once when the cell phone died and another time from a pay phone until he ran out of change. He was really trying hard to reassure me that he wanted to maintain contact.

No matter. My infantile emotions were raw by about 5:00 A.M. the following day when I awoke in a sweat and began piecing together the events of the previous day in a protective bout of analysis. My crafty brain dissected everything he had said to me the day before. I judged everything, from his motive for not charging his cell-phone battery to his lack of adequate coins in his pocket. Luckily, at the moment when I was ready to explode into anger, I heard his wise voice in my head. In the previous few weeks he had given me a reality check about my awful habit of psychoanalyzing every situation, telling me that it put a wall between the two of us. His advice: Stop thinking and start feeling. (Of course, my rebuttal included a directive for him to stop feeling so much and start thinking a bit more.)

In any event, on that anxious morning I took his advice to heart. I stopped thinking about him, his motives, his phone calls, his inconsistencies and instead focused on the emotions that were rising in me. *Shocked* is not the word for what came next. As I took a few deep breaths, as I paid attention to the tensions in my body, as I let myself be enveloped in feeling, I was overcome by a sickening feeling of fear. At the bottom of my mountain of lies was simple, deep-seated fear. I was afraid of rejection. And worse, I was afraid to get so close to someone that they might see this irrational fear.

I sat with my emotions for a few hours, during which time I placed two calls to my therapist. I talked to the Christmas Eve guy (finally!) at about 10:30 A.M. and was surprised at my reaction when I heard his voice. I felt a sense of calmness mixed with relief and I broke down in a gush of tears. I was a sobbing maniac on the phone as I talked to him about my fears. And I was even more surprised by his reaction. He told me to take a deep breath and he assured me that everything was okay. He wasn't defensive because I wasn't attacking him. He didn't reject me for my honesty; he rewarded me for it. We went through both our busy schedules for that day and planned for two separate times when we could talk again. He was clearly reassuring me. I spent the rest of the day feeling like I had had a chiropractic adjustment of my brain. I had not been wired for such a positive reaction. I think in the past, since I feared, though ignored, my feelings of rejection, I defended against them by living a dishonest experience. I would have acted cool with an angry edge—at least that's how he described me. Back then, I knew I had anger, but couldn't fathom the source. Being aware of my true feelings helped me get closer to someone.

QUESTION #5

Do you dream about a committed future with every man you date?
It's the stuff of fairy tales that makes reality so tragic.

Now here's where we get into the notion of unhealthy projections. It's a practice that runs rampant among women in our culture. We put a fairy tale ending on every encounter. The danger with these fantasies, of course, is that they will never live up to reality, not because we dream too high, but because we are only one half of a two-sided story. Who knows? Maybe sometimes we dream too low and unconsciously make *that* into a self-fulfilling prophecy.

The work of intimacy is to stay in the here-and-now as much as possible. That means we can make plans about when we'll talk to him next or when we'll see him next, but we should go gingerly about topics like nesting and long-range life goals. Those subjects in the early stages of dating can create relationship land mines. By doing this we are unconsciously conveying to him what our fantasy of him is and he, because he wants to be liked, will collude with us and make promises that he may not be able to keep.

Sometimes this dating phenomenon is impossibly cute. As a guest on an NBC talk show, *The Other Half,* I was asked to talk about the subject of dating lies. One couple in the audience told a story of their early courting, when the woman mentioned that she liked to skydive. (Was she really saying she needed a partner to skydive?) Her date responded by saying that he *loved* to skydive. Fast-forward to three months later when this woman "surprised" him by paying for a skydiving trip for his birthday. I suspect that, in their case, intimacy was built when he became honest about his fear of heights and his desire to impress her, by telling a big fat lie on that early date.

At other times, projections can be damaging. I once sat in a Las Vegas bar with a hunky television actor who obviously wanted to start a relationship with me. When I asked him to tell me about why his last relationship broke up, he very honestly told me that since he was often far away on sets, the distance made a close relationship impossible. He was clearly warning me and I refused to see this. I chose to invent the scenario that it was "she" who couldn't wait for "him." I decided that I was different. I could be long-distance monogamous. I could endure the e-mail/fax/phone relationship thing. I projected on the relationship a romantic jet-set love affair. Boy, was I filled with sobs when the tabloids gave me a reality check about his behavior abroad. He had been warning me about his inability to stay committed, and I slayed myself by my own projections.

Now, staying away from future projections and living in the moment doesn't have to happen forever. But in the first few months it's crucial to building trust and an honest experience. Talk about the feelings he evokes in you today, not the dreams for tomorrow.

Can you tolerate the wisdom in silence?
If you're always filling the space between you and your man, you may be crowding him out.

No doubt about it. We are the verbal gender. We console. We cajole. We iterate. We reiterate. We expel and expound. We glorify the world with a wealth of words. And most men, most of the time, are quite grateful that we take the tension out of silence.

But too much noise lets them off the hook. Remember it's their job to be 50 percent of the dynamic, at their own pace and in their own way, of course. But how can they participate if we don't give them room?

I think it is the project of many women to learn to tolerate silence. The obvious way is to allow pause to happen naturally in conversations. Don't rush to rescue him if he seems uncomfortable. From that discomfort will come jewels of wisdom. Sometimes enduring silence means being okay if he doesn't call you back as quickly as you'd like. Sometimes it means just waiting for his words. Sometimes it means paying attention to the other ways that he communicates—with body language, with touch, with metaphor. If you're truly listening instead of talking, you might find rich messages in the subtext of his stories.

For instance, a newly divorced man told a friend of mine that he knew he needed to concentrate on the long-term potential of his business, but he was being overwhelmed by the exciting transactional opportunites that, though they wouldn't lead to long-term profit security, were giving him a quick payoff. Was he really saying that he was having a lot of fun dating and having sex, even though he knew most of these relationships didn't have long-term potential? She took it as an apology for why he was moving so slowly with her. And she was right.

QUESTION #7

Are you woman enough to state your needs?
Are you even aware of your needs?

Paying attention to your feelings is a start in having an honest relationship. Defining your needs that result from those feelings is the other half of the equation.

Maybe you need a shoulder to cry on. Maybe you need lots of contact. Maybe you need your own space sometimes. Maybe you need time with your supportive girlfriends. Maybe you need a little less sports blaring in the house. Maybe you'd like a little less of his boys' club in your life. Maybe you need a few more candlelit dinners. Maybe you need for your man to make more decisions than you. Maybe you need to have a strong voice in all matters. Maybe you just need your man to take out the garbage.

Whatever it is, you cannot expect him to be a mind reader. You've got to identify and articulate your needs with clarity and conviction.

Now most of us deny even recognizing our own needs because we fear that if our neediness surfaces, it will chase people off faster than you can say, "Victim! Run!"

But the truth is a different story. I did hear men in my research describe "needy" women, but they were women who were over-the-top victims, women who expected men to satisfy every one of their whims, however infantile. Women who didn't take care of themselves. But for the most part, men welcomed the honesty of a vulnerable woman and felt safer to disclose themselves when a woman disclosed first.

According to one 24-year-old man from Nevada, "Every woman needs things. She needs attention. She needs to feel loved, wanted, and even needed. But as long as she doesn't 'need' my attention twenty-four hours, seven days a week, it's more than okay to be needy."

Most men agreed that women who were aware of their own needs and stated them clearly were much easier to deal with than women who slyly manipulated men and used passive-aggressive ways to get their way. One woman I know had a terrible fear of flying post–September 11. The problem was that her new heartthrob had invited her to fly to London just one month after the attacks. Instead of owning up to her fear and rescheduling the trip, she simply "forgot" to renew her expired passport. That's called being passive-aggressive. Most people don't even realize they are doing it, but unspoken emotions will sabotage a relationship every time.

QUESTION #8

Are you ready to be a fair financial partner?

Fair may not mean equal, but it means being equally responsible.

I think women are hypocrites when it comes to the topic of fair distribution of expenses. We want to be fair financial partners and have a voice in how expenditures are made, but we also think it's fair for a man to pay for more things (even if he makes the same or a little less than we do), and, boy, do we squawk when we have to ante up some cash.

Granted, you could make a case that since it's a little harder for women to make a lot of money in our culture, we like to hold onto it. Or that we take such a financial hit during our childbearing years when we are unable to work long hours and our expenses double, that financial security becomes a priority for us. I hear ya, girlfriends. I'm with you on that one. But let's assume that you and your dates are childless peers, both building your careers. Why should you assume, after the first few dates, that he should pay for everything, or even most things?

In her book *The Road to Wealth,* Suze Orman recommends that contributions to the union should be proportional to your respective salaries. In other words, if you make 20 percent more, you should be paying 20 percent more of the bills. But in the early stages of dating, when a man is doing the courting— and impressing—I do think it's okay to let him splurge on you. After all, he's investing in his future.

The greater point I'm trying to make here is, are you really ready to be a fair financial partner? Or, are you just taking advantage of his courting splurges until he runs out of expendable cash? Are you believing he's as rich as he pretends to be at this stage? I promise you he's not. He's just doing an age-old dance of displaying assets. It's no different from your Victoria's Secret Miracle Bra. You are just displaying your assets, which aren't quite as pretty when gravity checks in.

Being a fair financial partner means coming to honest terms with what you're looking for in a financial mate and how much you're ready to add to a prospective union. For instance, it does no good to date financial peers if you're going to run off with the first wealthy man who comes along. Likewise, it does no good to date rich men if you think they are trying to control you with their money. It's also fruitless to date hunky, great-in-bed, hardworking, blue-collar men if you're always going to think of them as financial failures.

You've got to figure out who you are. What you want. And how much you're willing to pay for it. Are you ready to be really responsible with money?

Do you fear rejection so much that you don't date risky men?
Love is a gamble—a scary wager where the losses or gains can be enormous.

Okay, here I am with another huge confession. It's particularly huge for me because it's something that I only recently became aware of. It's still sitting a little awkwardly in my consciousness while I judge the ramifications of the news. Anyway, enough of a preamble apology. Here goes:

In order to protect my heart, I have allowed myself to become vulnerable with only men who are "safe." What I mean by safe is, men who may feel less than me, whose identity and self-esteem are linked to my adoration of them, men who are controllable. Men with heaps of self-confidence, on the other hand, are terrifying to me. I usually find ways to sabotage things when those gentlemen come a callin'.

Other safe choices for me have included men who are emotionally avoidant, who don't put a lot of pressure on me to "put out" emotionally—while giving me the luxury of getting to blame them for the lack of intimacy in our relationship. And I also cling to men who are financially or intellectually inferior.

In fact, there is only one man in my entire 25 years of ovulation who was a risky love for me. He was smart. He was gorgeous. He was self-confident. He was tall. He made as much money as I do, and he was just as scared of intimacy.

What a crazy, dangerous combination. Our sometimes friendship, sometimes relationship was on and off for a decade while we boarded and then leaped off love's roller coaster. Talk about highs. Talk about lows. Do I regret it? Do I think I wasted my time? Hell, no! Remember the saying, "It is better to have loved and lost than to never have loved at all." Of course, I didn't marry this man. Didn't have a baby with him. Didn't cohabit. Didn't enter into a mortgage with him. Didn't get a tattoo with him. We never seemed ready for those traditional kinds of commitment.

But we certainly learned how to take risks with love. With him, I learned to be vulnerable with a true peer. I learned to be honest with a man. He was my boot camp relationship that helped me practice healthy relationship habits. If I could risk rejection by him, I knew I could do it with anybody. I am glad that I have known real love in this life and taken the risks associated with it.

Are you having a healthy relationship with yourself?
You are born with your own company. You will die with your own company. This is the big relationship of your life.

It took me so long to understand the difference between selfishness and self-love. Selfishness is for people who don't love themselves, who don't feel lovable, who scream for attention because it wasn't there when they were infants. They create a kind of insatiable need for consoling. Whether they are consoling themselves with money, clothes, cars, drugs, or bodies, it is no different from a toddler with a pacifier that can easily slip from her lips and reveal an unmitigated longing.

Self-love is something entirely different. It is care for your body and your soul. It is about creating a core of self-esteem that can only be rattled so much by the outside world. Self-love means appreciating your good qualities and also loving the things in you that you would like to change. They are all part of the mysterious mix of cells and soul that make you the unique and lovable person that you are.

So, are you having a healthy relationship with yourself? Do you treat your own body and spirit with compassion? Have you ever written yourself a love letter? (Truly. You should try it.) Do you know your own boundaries and how to erect them safely?

Do you understand your own emotional needs? Can you talk about your feelings? Do you love yourself even when you are crying?

If you answered *no* to too many of these questions, I implore you to focus on personal growth. Try an ethical therapist. Take a weekend workshop dedicated to internal awareness. Join a New Age church or find new meaning in age-old scriptures. Simply put, find your soul. You'll need it in every relationship with a man and you'll need it to relate to the most important person in your life—you.

the meeting & hooking-up test

5

> I had been looking for love, but only under specific conditions. . . . I had standards. It was just likely that my standards eliminated a number of possibilities.
>
> MAYA ANGELOU, WOULDN'T TAKE NOTHING FOR MY JOURNEY NOW (1994)

Okay, enough with the gentle exercise in self-awareness. Now it's on to the real test. Get your pencils ready because this one is scored. If you are currently single or have been dating someone for less than six months, use this and the other chapters of this five-part test to identify your own piece in the health of your relationships. If you're having trouble meeting men or getting them to call, think long and hard about the questions in this chapter, because, girlfriends, these are the basics of meeting and hooking up with a handsome honey.

QUESTION #1

Are your visual cues rejecting men?
"I don't approach a woman who is cold and standoffish. Her energy has to be welcoming."
—Man, 32, New York

So what the heck is *welcoming energy*? Should we be meditating and align our energy with the stars before heading out to the bars? Should we ensure that our moon is in the hospitality house before going to a house party? How the heck *do* we become a girlfriend welcome wagon?

While pondering all these questions, my friend Jodie came to mind. Jodie is the shining example of welcoming energy. I can't go anywhere with that girl without being crowded by men (and women, for that matter). In fact, she is such a reliable people-magnet that one year I took her to my company Christmas party, with three thousand employees and their spouses, and met more people in my company that night than I had met in the entire two years I had worked there—because Jodie introduced them to me.

So how does she do it? Well, let's start with what she doesn't do. Her arms are never, ever folded across her chest. She never clings to her shoulder bag for dear life. She never stands near any wall, but always seems to find the center of the room—with the best lighting, too! Her teeth are always on display in an engaging smile and when she catches someone's eye, she makes them feel like she's their best friend. Best of all, she's the queen of small talk. She finds a conversational jewel that will connect her to anyone. And, by the way, she plays that six-degrees-of-separation game better than anyone I know. A welcoming line might go something like, "I knew [so-and-so] from Aspen years ago. I heard he's one of your partners in this venture."

But back to body language for a moment. Even if you're an introvert who can't bear to be the center of attention, you could at least straighten those rounded shoulders and try to make eye contact with someone—anyone. The first few men will be practice targets while you get comfortable with the feeling of sending welcoming energy. The simplest pact you need to make to yourself today is, no more slouching into oblivion and smile, smile, smile.

Are you more worried about your appearance than your disposition?

"I like a woman with a good personality."
—Man, 24, New Hampshire

It's an old joke among men that when a guy says he likes a woman's personality, he really means she's not physically attractive. But notice that the subtext of this joke suggests that men, when presented with a classically unattractive woman, will find something attractive about her—like her interior beauty.

But with all joking aside, I did hear many men mention "personality" when asked what things repel or attract them to a woman. Such simple wisdom as "being nice" was heard a lot. Knowing how important kindness and intelligence is to men, I wonder if we women take too much advice from fashion magazines and not enough from psychology books.

Of course the billion-dollar cosmetics and fashion industry is there for one reason: It works. Men are visual animals and respond to heightened visual cues. Personally, my world is a different place when I venture out with makeup and a skirt than when I schlep around bare-faced in my sweats.

However, my research showed that most men don't like to approach women who wear too much makeup, or high fashion they don't understand, or who smoke. And they seem to hate really fake-looking boobs. (I didn't say they hate fake boobs. They just hate *really fake*-looking boobs.)

The big, giant, amazing fact about my survey is that not one man whom I interviewed mentioned weight. Not a one. Yet I think we women spend most of our time obsessing about our weight. Remember, the directive to be thin comes from fashion designers who want a nice hanger for their creations, not men who want a cuddly body and a warm womb for their bambinos. Anthropological studies around the world show that men look for a wide waist-to-hip ratio (curves) when choosing potential mates, not overall slimness. One man whom I interviewed summed it up beautifully. "I don't like Twiggy," he said. "What man wants to sleep with a bone rack?"

Science confirms the fact that personality counts a lot in the battle of the bathroom scale. A study from the University of Central Florida asked men to rate photos of women for their attractiveness. The full-body photos ranged from very thin to obese. One group was given a positive adjective that described the woman's personality, another group a negative adjective, and a third group was given no information at all about the women they were asked to judge. Surprise, surprise. When a man thought a woman was also "nice, kind, funny, or smart," her body weight didn't matter so much. Men who were given positive personality descriptions found a much wider range of women to be attractive.

Again it comes down to working on our interior selves and letting go of the negative value we place on looks.

Do you use rejecting behaviors when needed?

"Cut me off. Move away. Go to the bathroom. Pretend you have to go meet someone, but don't mislead me."

—Man, 27, California

Women send way too many "come hither" signals and confuse the hell out of men. This is according to a study from Vienna's Ludwig Boltzmann Institute for Urban Ethology. In the study, pairs of men and women, both strangers to each other, were placed alone in a waiting room with the thought that they were there to rate videos. The experimenter left the room for 10 minutes to take a phone call while hidden cameras rolled on the couple's interactions. Researchers later examined the footage for women's courtship signals such as hair flipping and head tossing and rejection signals for both parties, such as closed body language and avoiding conversation. Later both participants were asked to rate their waiting-room companion for overall attractiveness and their own interest level in dating that person. What was surprising is that, despite their body language, women weren't actually attracted to most of the men they were "flirting" with! Women, it seems, are really bad at sending out rejection signals. Are we that insecure that we need the attention of *all* men?

This is obviously not a good habit if one is a committed, monogamous girlfriend, but it's also not advantageous for a single woman. For your own sanity, and the sanity of the men around you, you need to become conscious of your behavior and the power you have to attract the right man rather than just any man.

A word for the wise from Beverly Hills matchmaker Dianne Bennett: If you don't reject the men you're not attracted to early on, then they will tie up all your time at a party or a bar. "Before you know it," says Bennett, "the night will be over and you've spent the whole time talking to losers."

Bottom line: The men I talked to hated women who were misleading and felt they spend way too much time deciphering women's mixed messages. So keep your signals clear and aim them at the right person for you.

QUESTION #4

Are you dating someone already?
"If she doesn't mention a boyfriend or husband in the initial conversation, then I assume she's single."
—Man, 38, Texas

This question, on face value, seems like the "Duh!" question from *The Boyfriend Test* that reads, "Does he have a girl-friend?" Of course, one assumes that if he's approaching you, or vice versa, that the two of you are completely available. But as you know from dating men who conceal the truth, that is not always the case.

It doesn't pay to hide the fact that you're dating someone else. The later a man finds out, the more hurt, angry, and betrayed he will feel. On the other hand, if you're doing the emotional work involved with closing a relationship, and you happen to meet Mr. Wonderful before all your loose ends are neatly tied up, then tell him so. He may ask that you wait and call him when you're available, or he may choose to see you only for a platonic lunch, but he probably won't go away entirely. This way, you can both have an honest experience from the start.

I heard plenty of stories from the men in my interviews about "the jerk she was dating when they met, whom he saved her from." Men are not afraid of a little competition, but they do like an honest, open, fair playing field.

QUESTION #5

Do you know how to show interest in someone?

"I know a woman is interested when she keeps wanting more info from me."
—Man, 21, Colorado

This is the part of the test where our elevated verbal skills can serve us well. Women are naturally good talkers and, I think, have inquiring minds. So inquire away. Men get the message that you're interested if you ask lots of questions about them. One word of caution, however: They told me they are not big fans of women who ask about their jobs only in terms of success level or ability to move up. They want women to ask how their work satisfies them or is special now, not its opportunities for advancement and ultimately a bigger paycheck.

And they don't like criticism and competition. Dianne Bennett says that men get criticism and competition all day long in their professional lives and they want a woman to bring relief from their struggles. The early stages of hooking up should never involve competition.

Do you know how to mirror the level of conversation?

"Don't be Zen-like if I'm being flippant and fun, and don't be silly if I'm having a deep conversation."

—Man, 28, Illinois

This wisdom came from only a couple of the men I interviewed, but their keen awareness of the dynamics of social interaction was profound. Let's talk about how conversational mirroring works. When you are approached by a man at a function, or you approach a man, or you are introduced to a man, you can quickly examine his demeanor to get cues of where his headspace is at that moment. Maybe you've eavesdropped on part of his conversation, maybe he mentions that he and his friend were just talking about a particular subject, or maybe you just visually take the emotional temperature on his face. Then you match his conversational tone and unwittingly send the message that you understand him.

Conversational mirroring shows that you're smart enough to pick up on social cues. It shows that you're flexible enough to adjust to any level of conversation, and it shows that you're interested in him and what he has to say.

The flip side are women who enter a dynamic, oblivious to what's going on, and do a sort of performance designed to get the man to join them in their charade. It's jarring. It feels uncomfortable and, according to men, can be downright annoying.

So open your eyes and ears and intuition, and you will start to connect to men in a more respectful way.

Do you know how to verbally reject a man without hurting his ego?

"There's only one line that helps ease the pain of rejection."
—Man, 34, California

I asked every man I interviewed how they would like a woman to verbally give them the brush-off and I got this answer over and over again: *"Sorry, I have a boyfriend."*

This is truly a safe way for men to be rejected. If they perceive that another man is in the picture, they can save face by being the gentleman and gracefully make an exit. So, don't tell them they are too young or too old for you. Don't tell them that you're not dating right now while you mend a broken heart. Don't tell them you're really busy with work. All these excuses present a welcome obstacle for men to overcome. It leaves them an opening they feel, as pursuers, they must take. Finally, after "revealing" the fact that there is a boyfriend in the picture, you must back up your words with body language by closing the conversation and moving away.

Are you confident enough to go out alone?

"I hate women who travel in packs. It's too much work to divide and conquer."
—Man, 26, New York

Oh, the horror stories I heard about the jealous "girl's girl" who prevented men access to their dream babe while the dream babe was oblivious to the subversive tactics of her girls' club comrade.

Apparently, this subject is hot in the trenches of the men's club. They moan about the girlfriends of the object of their attraction as if these women were an evil barrier between them and their love-of-the-moment. When my first book came out, I appeared on the ABC show *Politically Incorrect with Bill Maher*. It was a special episode for Valentine's Day called "Emotionally Incorrect," and during the half-hour Maher devoted most of the time to grilling me about what he brazenly called "c__k-blocks," women who, according to him, are worse than condoms for protecting the vagina from semen.

I understood the problem for men, but I didn't know the alternative. Were we supposed to be marching out to restaurants and clubs completely alone? The answer came with a resounding scream from that matchmaker whom I interviewed, Diane Bennett, *"Yes!"*

What a frightening, and maybe even dangerous, thought. I had to reconcile this advice with my own urge to protect women. After all, being alone, in seductive attire, in a room full of men and alcohol just isn't my idea of a safe time. So here are the Wendy rules for going out alone:

1. Never bring a friend to a house party. You've got the companionship of the hosts if you need it.

2. At restaurants, plan to meet a friend and simply arrive at least an hour earlier than he or she does and have a drink or appetizer.

3. In bars, always sit at the bar so you have the companionship of the bartender and so you can move if you get hounded by a loser.

4. If you are out alone, choose a bar or restaurant (if you can) that has valet parking so you don't have a dark, lonely walk to your vehicle late at night.

5. Attend happy hours near business centers as after-work crowds might be safer than late-night crowds.

6. If you are alone in a late-night bar, leave by 11:30. Nothing great happens after that hour, anyway. Trust me. Your beauty sleep is more important, so get in bed by midnight, Cinderella.

Are you brave enough to approach him?

"I like it when women take the pressure off me a bit."
—Man, 29, North Carolina

Yes, men like it when we take any kind of mating stress off them. Just like us, they don't want to be hounded by a suitor who won't give up, but they are flattered if a woman comes over to talk to them.

And, as you know, girlfriends, corny pickup lines never work. The rules for approaching a man are the same rules I gave men in *The Boyfriend Test*. Catch his eye first. Take the long route to the ladies' room so he can see you move about and read your body language, and finally, when you get close to him, say simply, "Hi." You'll know by his reaction if you're being invited to stay. And, if he is being kind of cool and aloof, then move on, girlfriend. You may have struck out but you saved yourself the aggravation of standing by the bar all night wondering if he is going to come talk to you.

Do you know how to give him your number?

"When she asks for my number, I know she's never going to call."
—Man, 34, California

First of all, in a traditional courting fashion, it is up to the woman to give her number to the man. Most men feel they are being rejected if a woman refuses to give up her number and asks for his instead. They tell me we rarely call when we say we will. (Probably at about the same rate that they don't call when they say they will.)

But there are a few tricks to getting him to ask for your number and keeping control of your privacy when you do.

Let's start with the challenge of getting him to ask. In your early conversation, you can slyly find a common denominator that might be an opening for you two to get together. The possibility of business synergism is a great one, as is the mention of a favorite museum or hot play that you both want to see, or even a church service one of you recommends. Whatever it is, just show interest in wanting to "check out" his suggestion. So there's the opening. If the courting fantasy is to be completed, you must follow through with a date. Now, if he doesn't ask for your number when it's time for one of you to leave, you can hand him a card with your number and say, "I'd love to check out that thing we were talking about."

There's your opening. There's your follow-through. Now move on and forget about him until he calls.

There is another situation in which you might want to quietly slip a man your phone number, and that's when one of you is out with an opposite-gender companion. If he's with a chick, even if she could be his cousin, it's not a good idea to saunter up and introduce yourself; likewise, if you're with a guy, he won't be stopping by your table to see if it's your brother or not. But that doesn't prohibit you two from locking eyes across the room or bumping into each other in the bathroom line. If all the silent courting signals have been sent and received, when it's time for you to leave, then put on your brave wild-girl persona and brush past him on the way out, slipping your card into his hand.

I've done this before and it has worked every time. Curiosity killed the cat, and men are so damn curious about a mystery woman that they always call to investigate. And, since you don't know his name, it's really fun to hear the way he describes himself on your voice mail.

Finally, how do you protect your privacy from a stranger whom you can't really trust yet? I suggest that you never give out your home number. Who needs a down-the-road late-night booty call from a guy you hardly care about? Decide which number you feel most protected by—an office voice mail, a pager, a cell phone, and give out that number where you can screen calls.

And don't give him a wrong number or the number to a Viagra hotline. That kind of behavior is cowardly and cruel. If you don't want to give your number to a man, just say so. If you do, then find a way.

The Meeting & Hooking-Up
Score Sheet Grade Report

Note: Give yourself 50 points to start out with.
Subtract or add points based on your answers
below. Choose only one answer that best
describes your feelings. And, remember, be
honest with yourself!

1. Are your visual cues rejecting men?

_____ I usually stand with my arms crossed.
(–10)

_____ I prefer to stand near a wall so I can
lean. (–10)

_____ I never approach people. I wait for them
to talk to me. (–15)

_____ I stand near the food or bar where
everyone hangs. (+10)

_____ I find it really easy to talk to new people
and always find something to say. (+15)

_____ The motto of my night is, Smile,
circulate, and chat away. (+20)

**2. Are you more worried about your
appearance than your disposition?**

_____ I spend at least an hour on wardrobe,
makeup, and hair. (–10)

_____ Well packaged, well coiffed, and
enhanced by plastic surgery, I am the
ultimate Barbie Doll! (–20)

_____ I basically like the way that I look and
am excited about the idea of new
conversations. (+20)

3. Do you use rejecting behaviors when called for?

____ Always. I can't stand to talk to anyone who wastes my time. (+15)

____ Most of the time I'm good at getting rid of guys, but sometimes I can't decide if I like them or not. (−15)

____ I never want to hurt anyone's feelings so I end up talking to guys I'm not really attracted to. (−25)

4. Are you dating someone already?

____ Yes, but I like to play the field. (−20)

____ I'm in a relationship, but we're about to break up. (−15)

____ I'm not seeing anyone at all. (+15)

____ My romantic life is no guy's business. (−25)

5. Do you know how to show interest in someone?

____ I like it when men are mostly interested in me and ask me lots of questions. (−25)

____ I like to sound smart and be an expert on some subjects. (−15)

____ I like to ask questions. (+10)

____ I am curious about people and am able to listen and provide open commonalities in my own life. (+20)

6. **Do you know how to mirror his level of conversation?**

_____ What does that mean? (−25)

_____ I'm pretty good at picking up on social cues and fitting in. (+20)

_____ I prefer to dazzle him with a great story I've got to tell. (−15)

7. **Do you know how to verbally reject a man while also being kind?**

_____ I know I'm really bad at this. I'm better at disappearing. (−15)

_____ I'm practicing this and getting better at being honest and kind. (+10)

_____ I usually have a way of making it clear that I'm not interested, and if he's still persistent, I'm not afraid to be honest. (+20)

8. **Are you confident enough to go out alone?**

_____ No, never. I need my girls' club. (−20)

_____ I sometimes get to a bar early to wait for my friends and am nervous, though I endure it. (+10)

_____ I stop by happy hours all the time and make a new friend quickly. (+25)

9. **Are you brave enough to approach him?**

_____ Nope. He's gotta come to me. (−25)

_____ Sometimes, when I'm feeling confident, I find a way to enter a conversation while I pass by. (+10)

_____ I can walk up to anybody and introduce myself. (+20)

10. **Do you know how to give him your number?**

_____ No. I'm kinda shy. (−15)

_____ It takes effort, but I'm pretty good at making an excuse about why I need to give him my number. (+5)

_____ If I want a man to have my number, I always find a way. (+15)

Grading the Meeting & Hooking-Up Test

This grade is calculated by adding or subtracting the scores from all the questions.

Exceptional	90–100	**A+**
Excellent	80–89	**A**
Very Good	75–79	**B+**
Good	70–74	**B**
Satisfactory	65–69	**C+**
Minimum Pass	60–64	**C**
Failure	50–59	**F**

the first-date test

> Women like silent men. They think they're listening.
> MARCEL ARCHARD (1956)

Would you like to have dinner on Friday night?" Those fateful words, or something similar, are the lead-in to one of life's most complicated dances, the first date. First dates are the ultimate fantasy. You behave as the person you wish you were and, likewise, he gives an award-winning performance of the man he hopes to convince you he is.

So how do we cut through the mirage and sort out what is real and what isn't? Well, there are many sly questions that, when asked in an unobtrusive manner, can give you plenty of information about his real character. They are also important things to listen for when they come up. But all that information is in *The Boyfriend Test.* This is your test. *The Girlfriend Test* is about your supportive participation in the illusion and your ability to be pretty honest at the dinner table. Remember, this is how men test *us.*

First dates should be great; life with him doesn't get any better than this. The many men whom I interviewed also reminded me that women have a role in making first dates great. We women should not consider ourselves spectators but cooperative players in the romantic fantasy of a candlelit night.

QUESTION #1

Do you know how to suggest a venue?

"I hate it when women try to fit everything into one night and try to turn it into a make-or-break evening."
—Man, 28, New York

Boy, do we know how to test men. We tell them to pick us up on Friday night and then give them just enough rope to hang themselves. Then we sit back and watch his suicide with an admonishing tsk, tsk!

Well, girls, real women, according to men, help them create a great night. Women who are real girlfriend material make some affordable suggestions on what to do that also gives them information about who they are. Certified relationship coach Suzanne Blake, who has counseled hundreds of men, says men want some direction: "They complain that most women seem so wishy-washy. They want to please the woman and, in order to do this, they need to know what she likes."

So fire away. Tell him what you like to do. Don't make it too complicated or too expensive and don't schedule more than two venues into one night, say, dinner and a show. One man even told me that it helps him when women suggest a place that is fairly easy to get to with convenient parking. It shows she's considerate. Once you've made the suggestions, though, don't offer to make the arrangements. That's too controlling.

Finally, when things don't go as planned, like the restaurant was overbooked and you were forced to wait with him at the bar for an hour, don't make him the bad guy. If you've participated in the planning of the date, then the blame can be shared. In fact, this tiny rupture in the first-date fantasy may be a route to healthy repair and eventual intimacy. Be his comrade, not his evaluator, and you'll be sharing more than this night.

Do you introduce him to your cats (and your grandmother's antiques)?

"Stop with the tour. Let's get out the door."
—Man, 35, New Jersey

When a man comes to pick you up, do you think it would be great if he really liked your cats? And it would be very cool if he appreciated your embroidered throw cushions or designer kitchen?

I promise you, he may ogle over your nest another day, but a first date is not the time to drag him through the family photo albums or ask him to talk baby talk to your kitties. This is behavior that is far too familiar for strangers. And it puts on too much pressure.

Cats, it seems, are a hot button for men. Many of the men I interviewed worry if a woman has more than one cat and talks to them as if they were children. What is it about women and their cats? I dunno. I think men have visions of us becoming crazy cat ladies and eventually eliminating them.

I suggest that instead of the whole tour, meet him in front of your building or answer the door, grab your coat, and go. Don't linger too much at your place on a first date. He doesn't want to enter your fantasy. He wants you to enter his.

Do you talk too much?
"Stop selling yourself, 'cause— guess what?—I'm already on a date with you."
—Man, 35, Florida

Sometimes it is comforting to a man if the woman fills all the awkward silences with lively banter, but more often it is a put-off. Men want you to be interested in them, and they want to be heard. (Just as you do.) But all this selling of yourself isn't a two-way conversation. It's a competitive sales pitch. Plus, women communicate at a quicker pace than men, who feel they sometimes can't keep up. Says one man, "Women are such fast communicators and I feel like I'm getting stepped on all the time."

So here are some tips for healthy first-date communication: First of all, ask plenty of questions. Then give him time to answer. Men are not the verbal gender and need a few moments to think and formulate words. And don't interrupt until you're sure he's finished. His pause for a breath could be a bid to regroup, gather his thoughts, and continue. And finally, when his responses to your questions trigger stories about you, bite your tongue! Believe me, he'll get a chance in the future to hear every titillating detail about you and your life because you'll tell him. But don't dominate the first date with your own glowing reviews unless you're asked specifically.

Do you express jealousy?
"If she gets jealous, I only know it's going to get worse."
—Man, 24, Canada

I was a little bemused that a chunk of guys mentioned jealousy when asked what's the worst thing a woman can do on a first date. While it wasn't the absolute worst thing, according to my statistics, the subject of female jealousy cropped up enough times for me to give it a mention.

Apparently some women feel threatened if a man happens to glance at another woman, talk to a female friend, or talk about ex-girlfriends. Then they get in "snitty moods" for the rest of the evening.

Girlfriends, are we *that* insecure? Even if we are that insecure, why do we sabotage our fantasy first date by expressing it? Look, girls, he's on a date with you. He likes you, or he wouldn't be there. Cut him some slack and curb your feelings of jealousy.

Do you tell lies?

"Red lights for me: Not being herself. Not giving honest information. Hiding her relationship history."
—Man, 42, California

False eyelashes and a Botox forehead are acceptable lies. Control-top pantyhose is an acceptable lie. An omission about your current relationship status is not. Misleading statements about your job, your church-going habits, or your values are not acceptable lies.

Guys want to hear the truth, just as you do. They want you to open up first so they know it's a safe place for them. Of course I don't suggest that you hurt yourself if you don't think the guy is safe. Try small disclosures to test his empathy level and tell him honestly why you don't want to reveal certain information. It's up to you to find a comfort level between painful, humiliating honesty and a loving and authentic expression of who you are. Only you know where that place is. But the men in my research complained that women protected themselves so much that they didn't seem real or human. So, don't be afraid to lower your walls just a little in order to tolerate being honest. It's the only way to create a bridge to his inner self.

Do you control too much?
"Help me make it perfect, but don't steal my show."
—Man, 26, California

Suggesting a venue is a sweet way to help a guy out and to introduce him to you and your tastes. Taking control of the evening is a way to emasculate him. The ways that women control, according to the men I talked to, include making the reservation, providing transportation for him, announcing yourself to the host before he gets a chance to, speaking to the waiter on his behalf, and then insisting on a particular after-date activity.

If you're laughing at the picture of such a controlling woman with the attitude that this could never be you, listen to this. I was once having dinner with a man and we had just completed the conversation about whether to order dessert or go elsewhere. I clearly stated my preference to go elsewhere, which I think was okay, because it expressed my need, and we agreed on a late-night spot. When the waitress arrived and asked me if I'd like dessert, I should have simply declined and left a silence for him to ask for the check. But I was busy being efficient, not thoughtful, so in one breath I found myself declining dessert and asking for the check. The waitress gave my date a quizzical look and then asked *him* if he would like dessert or coffee. He chose to have some coffee, and I was so embarrassed. Did he decide to have the coffee to make the point that I was leading? Was it his way of taking control back?

This is clearly one of those issues of too much male energy at the table. So I advise you to leave your management skills at the office and find honor in being led. And I promise to take my own advice!

Do you talk too much about past relationships?

"Honestly, I hate to hear anything about ex-boyfriends. If she talks about them a lot (good or bad), I think she's not over them."
—Man, 30, Tennessee

This was a big one with men. It's important that we enter into their first-date fantasy all alone. No male baggage or, dare I say, issues need accompany us. If he asks about our relationship status, we might give him some simple facts about the most recent one to assure him it has ended, but he really doesn't want a complete relationship résumé.

So, don't think it impresses him to speak well or negatively of our past loves. Complimenting them may make him feel inferior and criticizing them may make him wonder if he'll be the next target for your sharp tongue. Be coy. Be cool. Be honest. And protect those former men who may also be growing at their own pace.

Do you neglect your own needs in order to be a good companion?

"This is huge. If the two get involved further, it will turn into, 'We always do things you want to do and never do the things I like.'"

—Man, 24, Nevada

I know that expressing your needs seems to contradict my advice to enter his fantasy and mirror him a bit, but I do think the two things are possible. Expressing your needs is different from insisting on them and executing them. For instance, if a guy invites you to a hockey game on a first date, it's perfectly okay to admit that you're not a hockey fan but are game to try something new. If it turned out to not be your favorite dating activity after all and he invited you on another occasion, it's up to you to remind him of your dislike of hockey and suggest something that you do like to do. That way, you can start laying the groundwork for reciprocity. The message you want to impart is that you're happy to make compromises for him if he reciprocates. These psychological systems can become quite binding down the road and are very difficult to change. It's important that you exert your needs from the very start of a relationship to help build a healthy, mutually satisfying connection.

Do you try to pick up the check?

"I'd think she was too independent and not too comfortable in a relationship."
—Man, 30, Illinois

There is only one reason to ever offer to pick up or split a first-date check and that is that you are not attracted to this man and never want to see him again. Men believe that this is the message they are being sent when this happens. Paying for our dates, as you'll read about in chapter 8, "The Girlfriend Sex Test," is one way to protect yourself from date rape, because this might reduce a potential perpetrator's feeling that the woman owes him something. But with a man who may have relationship potential, paying the check means you're not attracted to him and might send him running.

Please remember, even if he pays your check and tips the parking attendant for you, you owe this man nothing. He has paid for a small piece of your valuable time. You are a treasure at his table. He knows this, or he wouldn't have asked you out. Let him pay the check and thank him briefly and quietly. Don't gush forward with too much gratitude, or you'll send the message that you don't recognize your own value. Great girlfriends are gracious and confident and worth splurging on.

QUESTION #10

Do you push for sex?
"If she were a guy, I'd tell her to be a gentleman and keep it in her pants."
—Man, 36, California

I think we are finally beginning to reach a time of sexual equality when I hear so many men talk about the sexual aggressiveness of women. But, taking our cues from a model of male sexuality, we may have inadvertently adopted the behavior of bad boys instead of gentlemen. Nearly 90 percent of the men in my research confided to me that they really didn't want sex on the first date. They wanted a sexy good-night kiss to feed their hopes for a lusty sexual encounter in the future, and sometimes they feel pressured by women to go too far.

My advice, if you're feeling frisky at the end of a first date: Give him a smoldering good-night kiss. Don't linger too long in his car. Then head alone to your own bed to finish the job yourself. That's what a gentleman would do. And great girlfriends are the ultimate gentlemen.

The First-Date
Score Sheet Grade Report

Note: Give yourself 50 points to start out with. Subtract or add points based on your answers below. Choose only one answer per question. Pick the one that best describes your feelings. And, remember, be *honest* with yourself!

1. **Do you know how to suggest a venue?**

_____ I like a man to make all the plans. (–10)

_____ I am comfortable giving suggestions about where to go. (+10)

_____ I am comfortable making arrangements if he needs me to. (–15)

2. **Do you introduce him to your cats?**

_____ I love to show off my place and pets. (–10)

_____ I like to get out the door quickly. (+10)

_____ I use my pets as a test. If they don't like him, it tells me something. (–20)

3. Do you talk too much?

_____ When I'm nervous, I talk a lot. (+15)

_____ I think of myself as a good listener. (+15)

_____ I feel nervous around quiet men and want to fill the space. (−10)

_____ I get hurt if they don't ask a lot about me. (−5)

_____ I am very curious and love to ask questions. (+20)

4. Do you express jealousy?

_____ I think it is rude when a date looks at another woman. (−20)

_____ Looking is fine, but if he chats with another woman, it makes me crazy. (−10)

_____ I'm pretty confident and don't mind a little competition. (+15)

5. Do you tell lies?

_____ No, but I do omit facts sometimes. (−10)

_____ I think a little lying is okay. (−15)

_____ I never lie. I am blatantly honest. (−5)

_____ When I choose not to disclose, I tell him why. (+15)

6. Do you control too much?

_____ Subtract 10 points for each of the following true statements:

1. I want to choose the restaurant.

2. I want to drive my own car.

3. If I arrive first, I announce myself to the host or hostess.

4. I hate it when a man orders for me.

5. If I need something, I signal the waiter myself.

_____ None of the above apply to me. (+20)

7. Do you talk too much about past relationships?

_____ I think a guy should know what I've been through. (−20)

_____ I'm very secretive about my past. (−15)

_____ I answer questions when asked but don't volunteer info. (+15)

_____ I think it's nice when we can commiserate together about our most recent breakups. (−15)

8. Do you neglect your own needs in order to be a good companion?

_____ I'm really shy about expressing my desires. (−20)

_____ I want to know about him and his life, not talk about my boring activities. (−20)

_____ I hate to speak up so early in a relationship, so I wait a while. (−10)

_____ I like to set things straight from the beginning, so I tell him what I like. (+20)

9. **Do you try to pick up the check?**

_____ I hate owing a man something, so I always try to split the check. (–10)

_____ I offer only if I really don't like him. (+10)

_____ If I really don't like him, I make sure he pays. (–25)

_____ I'm comfortable with men splurging on me. (+20)

10. **Do you push for sex?**

_____ Never. (–10)

_____ If he's hot and I'm horny, I let him know. (0)

_____ If I want a long-term relationship with him, I choose to wait. (+20)

Grading the First-Date Test

This grade is calculated by adding the scores from The Meeting & Hooking-Up Test (page 86), and The First-Date Test (preceding). Then divide by two to get your average score. How are you faring so far?

Exceptional	90–100	A+
Excellent	80–89	A
Very Good	75–79	B+
Good	70–74	B
Satisfactory	65–69	C+
Minimum Pass	60–64	C
Failure	0–59	F

the five-date consis- tency test

> There's something every woman
> wants, and that's a man to blame.
> PHILIP ROTH, *THE COUNTERLIFE* (1987)

Breathe a sigh of relief, girlfriend. You met him. You charmed him. You accompanied him on a date or two. Now comes that gray area where you're more than a date, but far less than a girlfriend. This is a time of erratic emotions and lessons about learning to regulate those emotions. It's a time when fantasies about a future together can sabotage the reality of actually being together. It's a time when sex often happens and scares the bejesus out of one or both of you, and it's a time to test the waters of vulnerability. Can he be trusted with your tender spots? Are you trustworthy with his?

I personally think the three-to-five–date stretch is the most vulnerable time in a new relationship. At this point there has been so little investment of time, emotions, or finances by either party that it's really easy to call it quits if something feels threatening. It's also a time when fantasies about the future are still operating while real life is beginning to cast a shadow—something that could make either partner flee at a moment's notice.

So let's take a look at your piece of this. How might a girlfriend candidate activate fight or flight instincts in a man?

Are you physically available?

"I don't think I should have to wait seven to fourteen days to be fit into her busy schedule."
—Man, 43, Massachusetts

Here's a giant reality check, oh, proud career woman: At this point he probably doesn't worry about what you do for a living, how much money you make, or how much in demand you are at work. He cares only to see you. The thought that a career and busy life can increase our attractiveness in a man's eyes is projection on our part. That's what we care about when we evaluate *him.* Men, on the other hand, just want a woman to be content with herself (and possibly with her work) and available for him.

This revelation was shared with me over chardonnay by a girlfriend who is smart, beautiful, and a very, very busy, hugely successful attorney. She had recently started dating a wealthy man who was just ending a two-year relationship. When she happened to ask him where he met his ex-girlfriend, he said at a housewares store. "Oh, how cute," she responded, "were the two of you comparing blenders?"

"No," he replied, "she sold me my blender."

"Did she own or manage the store?" was my surprised friend's query.

"No, she just worked there," he said in a quizzical way that expressed wonder at why she would ask such a question.

Okay, so women may not date a guy who flips burgers and next date an investment banker, and then move to a public school teacher, just because they all seemed like nice guys. Most of us are much too material for that. We're much too status-conscious for that. (And, good for you, girlfriend, if you're not.) But most men aren't that way. They want an attractive woman with a great personality who is available, like every two to five days, and they don't care much what she does for a living, as long as she's happy and shows up for them.

Being the kind of woman who drops everything at the prospect of a hot date (usually, to my own detriment), I was really surprised to hear so many men complain about the scheduling problems they have with women. Is it really possible that our jobs are more important than our opportunities for an empathic connection? Wow. That one floored me.

So rule number one of the five-date test is, be available! Don't make a man wait a week or, God forbid, *two* to see you. I promise, while you're off on that all-important new business development trip, he's developing something of his own with a woman who's available. Who once said that half of life is just showing up? Anyway, they were right.

Are you emotionally available?

"The worst mistake that a woman can make in the first five dates is to be dishonest."
—Man, 29, Maine

I think that quote from a man in Maine had a deeper meaning than the obvious. While it's not okay to openly lie about some objective reality, it's also not okay to lie about your feelings, however trivial or embarrassing they may seem.

One man stopped seeing a great woman after just a few dates because he had a sense that she wasn't being authentic, although he couldn't quite put a finger on how. For example, on their second date, the subject of sushi came up. Making light conversation and attempting to find common ground, the man asked his date what kinds of sushi she liked to eat. She replied that she liked to eat California rolls. Then he pressed for more. Did she also like salmon or spicy tuna rolls? This man really wanted to get to know her, including her tastes. The woman smiled coyly and evaded the question by telling him she likes to hold her cards close to the chest. The subject was changed.

Their dating relationship ended soon after. Was the woman embarrassed that she really doesn't like to eat raw fish and orders California rolls because they are the only thing she can stomach in a sushi restaurant? The man never knew. The only message he got that night was, "I don't want you to know me." By being protective, she had had a dishonest experience with him. This conversation was probably one of a few that hinted that the woman didn't trust him, or didn't like herself, warts and all.

Now, having laid out a prescription for total honesty, I want to reiterate something I talked about in *The Boyfriend Test.* Sometimes, being honest means keeping your boundaries intact and explaining why in an open and nondefensive way. In the early stages of dating, you don't have to tell him that you had a mastectomy, or that you lost your virginity at twelve, or that you have a standing appointment at Weight Watchers on Wednesday nights. If subjects come up that might create an opening for this kind of information, it is still honest to say, "You're asking about information that I'm not ready to share with you. I like you a lot and hope that someday we'll reach a level of closeness and trust that are worthy of my most intimate thoughts. I hope you can respect that." The biggest part of that statement is the honesty about one's feelings. Pay special attention to these words: "I'm not ready," "I like you," and "I hope."

These statements show that you are aware of your own feelings, you know yourself, and you're self-confident enough to share your feelings. If you're not used to doing this, practice sentences that start with "I feel . . . " and then add the most fitting emotion. Here are some rehearsal words to follow "I feel":

> proud
> afraid
> confident

uncomfortable

happy

angry

connected

confused

secure

abandoned

attacked

loved.

I promise you that powerful communication like this is the most attractive thing a confident person can bring to the dating table. It sounds a lot more real than "I like to hold my cards close."

QUESTION #3

Are you already planning to change him?

"I hate women who ask if I'm thinking of getting a different job soon."
—Man, 30, Colorado

Man oh man, aren't we the controlling gender? We meet a perfectly decent fellow and by the third date have redesigned him in our heads. His dogs and cigars are out the window. His furniture has been rearranged, his wardrobe revamped, and his career under full makeover mode. Who do we think we are, God? On the eighth date, *she* created man?

One of the men I interviewed married a woman with a six-year-old child ten years ago. At the time, he was an aspiring stockbroker and she ran a small child-care facility in her apartment. He told me he had dated all kinds of super-career-oriented women and some serious babes, but the thing that made him settle down was the mutual respect he and his wife had for each other's goals. He respected that she wanted to do child care because she loved it, and she respected that he wanted to learn the trading business. Each of them had to make some sacrifices in order to support the other's goals—she had to put up with his early-to-rise, early-to-bed life and he had to put up with extra children at the dinner table when parents worked late. According to him, neither career was considered more valuable than the other. They simply respected each other.

He told me that was a huge contrast to the many other women he had dated who had tried to change him. I noticed that this man, along with the vast majority of the men I interviewed, used the word *controlling* a lot. Apparently, the female gender gets a lot of bad press in America for trying to change men. Hey, girls, maybe we should focus on changing ourselves instead. Just a thought.

Do you play phone games?
"Please, always call back!"
—Man, 33, New York

I can honestly say that the phone-game thing was the most commonly cited complaint that my men had about women. Let's start by defining what a phone game is, because there are many variations.

One game (that men are very good at, too) is the game of tag in which no one actually gets tagged. It involves calling his office voice mail when you know he's at home, or vice versa, or leaving a message on his cell phone when you know it's off, like when he's in church. In the latest revision to this game, you move from phone contact to e-mail and slowly stretch the duration between missives. So you're both continually leaving messages for each other, and no one is actually talking.

Women play that game of tag as much as men, but we have an even better, distinctly female, version. Since we are the verbal gender, we're not afraid of a little conversation, even if nothing honest is said. So, we sometimes take his call or e-mail and simply express dismay that we're not available on the particular evening he wants to take us out. Then we put men into that embarrassing position of trying again and again, hoping that one day they will "get the message" and stop calling. To play this game at an expert level, one former roommate of mine used to tell selective men she'd be out of town. Then, I'd watch in amusement while she ignored her ringing phone all week and constantly checked her voice mail. Of course, today caller ID helps such women immensely.

Finally, men tell me that some women play the don't-call-back game. If they're not interested, they just don't call back—ever. The hope here, I assume, is that the man won't try again—ever.

Back in my busy dating days when I was less secure and more unaware, I usually played the game of taking the call, though not being available. But on a couple of occasions, when I was swamped with work and other men, I remember doing the don't-call-back game. There is one man in particular for whom I still get a guilt pang in my heart whenever I think about it. I met him at Home Depot (great place to meet men, girls) and we had one roller-blade date at the beach. After that, the game of phone tag started and, because I was not confident, I just didn't call him back. The poor guy left about three messages on my machine in the course of a couple of weeks. He really took a while to "get the message." Then just as I was beginning to feel relief that the game was over, I saw him at a television news shoot that I was working on. The two of us were in eyeline, but not voice proximity, for about two hours. I felt so awful. I could feel his hurt from one hundred yards away.

Sadly, all telephone games are plain hurtful and dishonest. I think we have to learn to be brave women and just bite the bullet. The men in my research said they wouldn't mind if a woman told them she had hooked up with an old boyfriend or that she didn't want him to waste his time with her, since she wasn't looking for a relationship. Most of them seemed to agree that a conversation, almost any conversation, is better then leaving them hanging. Think of how we feel waiting by the phone. Men may not express it, but they have the same anxiety. So please, ladies, call a fella back and give him a kind brush-off, or be available for him. But don't be a flake.

QUESTION #5

Are you rewarding bad-boy behavior?

"We see great women get treated badly and seem to love it, so that's what we think we have to do."

—Man, 28, Pennsylvania

During my research the conversation often turned to the subject of bad-boy behaviors. I would be busy firing away my organized list of questions about women's behavior, and I guess I gave the impression that I was the dating guru (ha!), because the talk would somehow morph into questions about why women prefer bad boys. It seems to baffle nice guys that we could be so stupid.

I tried to explain to some of them about Attachment Theory and that anxiously attached women tend to prefer emotionally avoidant men because they mirror their early-life experiences. It's almost as if our brains were telling us that "this time we will make Daddy love us." But most guys ignored my analysis and simply said something like, "Well, bad-boy traps work, so I'll do it."

I was kind of amazed by that thought. Could it be that plenty of men out there don't have insecure attachment patterns at all? Instead, are their avoidant tendencies a learned behavior because it is deemed a successful tactic to obtain sex? That notion rocked my world. By rewarding bad boys, we women are setting the standards for onlookers. Men take their cues from men who seem successful at mating. They don't see kind, empathic men in action, because those guys are at home with us building a shelf for our shoes. They see jocks, actors, sexy nightclub owners, and guys on Harleys out at the bars juggling women and not being true to any of them. Simply put, it is the bad boys who are more visible and, therefore, role models for many young men.

So if we want to help women of the world, and ourselves, we have got to stop rewarding bad-boy behavior. Read *The Boyfriend Test* if you want some tips on how to choose better and to reject bad behavior early in a relationship. The bottom line: Reward kindness and it will flourish.

Can you wait by the phone and control your anxiety?

"I don't get why women are so angry if we take a while to call back."
—Man, 24, Illinois

Oh, the waiting. The waiting. I think the act of waiting for someone we like to call us back is probably one of the most excruciating pains a woman can feel—especially one who has a somewhat anxious attachment style. I know this feeling intimately because it was the battle cry that sent me into therapy. Okay, waiting for a call, or e-mail, or letter from a boyfriend who was seven seas away from me was part of my anxiety; the other was that I had not properly mourned the death of my parents. Both feelings, by the way, are part of the same thing—separation anxiety.

When a loved one (or an object of our infatuation) fails to call us back promptly, the feelings it triggers are as visceral as when a newborn child awaits Mommy's arms and breast. It is a horrible, frightening pain. It is the most basic and primal fear of a human being, the loss of another whom we think is part of ourselves.

And it is understandable. For in his presence we are transformed into the perfect woman. We feel beautiful. We feel smart. We feel funny. We feel sexy. We are the perfect date. Until the date ends and the days of waiting for his call start.

Then who do we become? A sad date? A lonely date? An unworthy date? The reigning question in our minds is, "Why doesn't he feel as happy in our presence as we do in his?" But that is only the first stage of separation anxiety. It gets worse.

Next we beat ourselves up by reliving the date in our heads and finding fault with our own behavior. Well, if I hadn't said this . . . if I hadn't been clumsy about that . . . if I had worn something different . . . then maybe he would call.

Then we hit the angry stage of separation anxiety. We take all those unfair criticisms of ourselves and transfer them to him and become angry. I can't tell you how often my anxiety-ridden head has screamed, "He's messing with me! He knows how much this hurts and he's doing this deliberately to put me at a disadvantage!" Separation anxiety has become anger, just as it did to the infant left at the crib to cry alone.

Sometimes our anger becomes so extreme that we blanket it across the entire male species. When one guy doesn't call, we hate 'em all. If you're like me, you might have even fantasized the wish that one of your trusted girlfriends would grow a penis, so you could marry her and be sexually satisfied too. This anger stage is a hard one, girl. I've lived through it enough times to tell you, it ain't pretty.

The final stage of separation anxiety has two paths. The first one is easy though not growth enhancing. The second is painful though truly helpful.

The first path is one of protection. We vow to never become too intimate with a date ever again. We learn to hide our feelings. We shut down just a little. Instead of feeling the pain of separation, we focus on self-consoling acts like shopping, gossiping, working out, eating (or not eating), working, or, my personal favorite, pursuing other men. We replace the feelings of abandonment with artificial feelings of beauty, health, and prosperity. Do this enough times with enough rejecting men, and you will become a nonfeeling android. I promise.

By the way, should your date call back during this stage, you will be too protective and less emotionally available—and ultimately less attractive to him. Separation anxiety can be so self-sabotaging.

The second path involves connecting with a surrogate figure whom you really trust. A close girlfriend, a therapist, your children, if you have them. If you've been able to allow yourself deep feelings of connection within these kinds of strong relationships, then you will be reminded of your value simply by being in their presence. Now, I'm not suggesting that you tell your child about your broken heart—children are too young to handle that emotional burden—but spending some quality time with one who regards you as omnipotent is a great path to healing.

Finally, after the passing of time, along with maybe some deep meditation and/or some fortifying therapy, you will start to feel good about yourself again—without him. What a great feeling that is. Complete self-esteem without the approval or adoration of another. It is a state of self-love. You're back. Phew!

Then he finally calls. And after some time feeling satiated and another date, the whole cycle can start all over again. We can again become an object of *his* love, not ours.

So how do we keep from losing a part of ourselves every time a man doesn't call back? How do we not let our dates walk away with the best part of us while we wait, with an amputated heart, by the telephone? The only way is to create deep intimacy in the other relationships in our lives—with our girlfriends, our siblings, an older, wiser friend, our children, and our therapists. Know that you are loved and lovable, and in times of vulnerability, these loving relationships will remind you of that.

Then pick up the phone or send him an e-mail, telling him how much you enjoyed him.

QUESTION #7

Can you pick up the phone when you need to?

"I can't stand a woman who suffers from dial-itis. It puts too much pressure on me."
—Man, 35, Washington

This is a different form of the telephone game. The habit of not calling (or rarely calling) men can be one of three things. It is either a tactic to endure our separation anxiety, through gritting our teeth while reciting the mantra, "I can wait it out. I can wait it out." Or, it is some kind of old-fashioned game of playing hard-to-get in order to create anxiety in him. Or, worst of all, it is a test to see how much he likes us. Some women use the frequency of his calls as the barometer of their self-worth.

Well, girls, here's my advice, throw out that tattered copy of *The Rules* and pick up the phone. If he isn't interested, you'll get the message a whole lot quicker than through the waiting game. If you miss him, call him, and tell him so. If you get no response, then you've got your answer. He's not into you. So move on. Somebody else will be into you. Or, if you find that he runs away because you're calling too much and smothering him, then you will learn to regulate better. But you'll never learn to regulate your feelings if you're at home staring at the phone and gritting your teeth.

QUESTION #8

Are you pushing your family and friends on him already?

"I don't want to meet her family for at least a month, but I can meet a friend or two after about three dates."
—Man, 33, California

There was some variation on the answers I got to the question "When do you want to meet her friends and family?" Some men, lovely, old-fashioned, and probably young guys, are happy to meet parents on the first date. Others wanted a private courting period for a month or two. Still others seemed kind of open to meeting friends through some kind of group event, but only after at least three or four dates.

There were such a wide variety of responses that I think the most important information a woman needs to get is what effect meeting the clan can have on a man. Ask him about what he's comfortable with. If he seems resistant, at all, then know that such introductions have great meaning to him. And just because he's not ready to meet your friends and family doesn't mean he won't ever be ready. Be patient. Wait. Talk about it gingerly. And, above all, don't spring any surprise visits on him.

I did that once to a man who was very emotionally avoidant. Remember, people avoid because they are extra sensitive. I simply brought my roommate out to the car when he was picking me up for a date. He was not pleased and his game of emotional retreating became more pronounced after that. I should have been aware of his state of readiness before springing her on him.

The best move is to talk about why he's uncomfortable meeting your friends. If he can talk about his feelings, then he's got potential. But pushing your family on him before he's ready is disrespectful.

Are you aware of how your menstrual cycle can sabotage relationships?

"I still don't get this PMS thing. I think it's a good excuse for a bad mood."
— Man, 22, Connecticut

Premenstrual syndrome, as it turns out, is *not* the biological land mine that can wreak havoc in a budding relationship, and I've got science to back me up on this one. I recently came across a study from the University of Bamberg in Germany called "Jealousy, General Creativity, and Coping with Social Frustration During the Menstrual Cycle." I couldn't wait to read that one.

And fascinating it was. The researchers tested women's sensitivity to feelings of jealousy during three phases of the menstrual cycle, using biofeedback instruments not unlike a lie detector test. With the machines recording data, female participants listened to stories and imagined situations that involved (a) nonsexual jealousy where their partner forms a deep emotional attachment to another woman, (b) sexual jealousy where the partner has sexual intercourse with another woman, and (c) no jealousy, stories of social interaction lacking emotional connections.

The results were illuminating. Stories of nonsexual jealousy, a complete loss of the partner's emotional investment, caused the most reaction during the preovulatory phase. Stories of sexual jealousy caused the most distress during the ovulatory phase. From an evolutionary point of view, this all makes sense. Who wants her partner flirting with another woman just before her eggs are ready to be fertilized and, worse, who wants her man sharing sperm when her egg is waiting in her own fallopian tube? What was most interesting to me is that the premenstrual phase wasn't the most dangerous time for feelings of relationship insecurity.

The whole idea shed new light on a bout of jealousy I once had. The situation was this: A dreamy man and I were in the early stages of a hot romance when he told me that an old friend from college, named Connie, was coming to stay at his place. Now, I like to play the part of progressive woman who believes that platonic friendships between men and women can take place, although my internal code sings a different tune, so I simply said, "That's cool."

Well. During the week that "Connie" was in town, my man seemed to rarely check in with me. And my brain went into disaster mode. I couldn't stop thinking about the sleeping arrangements in his one-bedroom apartment. He had an uncomfortable, U-shaped leather couch that no man or woman would ever attempt a night's rest on, so all I could picture was female company in his king-size bed. I was filled with anxiety. I was a wreck. I even took this one to therapy. In hindsight, maybe I should have checked my menstrual calendar to calm myself down a bit.

The punch line of this story is hysterical. A week after his houseguest had vacated (and I was in a more stable PMS stage), I found myself in his king-size bed. As I lay there I noticed a few large men's golf and dress shirts hanging on his door handle and asked if they were new.

"No," he said, "Connie left them here. He always leaves a trail behind."

"Connie?" I asked, trying to conceal the crack in my voice. "What kind of name is Connie for a man?"

"I guess it's short for Conrad, but nobody calls him that."

I was shocked. I was embarrassed. I felt like a complete fool. My intuition had let me down and I risked damaging the precious trust that he and I had been attempting to create. So, girls, when you feel jealous, never make assumptions and always check the calendar.

QUESTION #10

Are your parenting skills respectful and empathetic?
"I can tell a lot about a woman's emotional makeup over the course of a few dates by watching her parenting skills."
—Man, 36, New York

I admit I had never thought to ask a question about parenting in a dating interview. I assumed that I was writing about single people, until many of my male subjects reminded me that many single people have children. So, whether they're his or yours, kids are a test for your relationship skills. I thought it pretty enlightening that more than a few men mentioned they can tell a lot about our down-the-road personality by how we treat kids, even if they are our nephews and nieces. Wow! They're really watching!

The big turnoff, according to men, was women who yell at their kids. Next were complaints about being too strict or too lax. Overall, the men told me they see parenting skills as an indicator of intelligence and a kind of blueprint for how they will be treated in times of stress. Other men, when asked what were the traits that attracted them to their wives, also included "good mother" in their list of accolades. Pretty clever guys. So girls, take a parenting class or spend some quality time with the younger members of your family. It might improve your datable quotient.

And that's the five-date test. Now it's time to test your score.

Five-Date
Score Sheet Grade Report

Note: Give yourself 50 points to start out with. Subtract or add points based on your answers below. Choose only one answer per question. Pick the one that best describes your feelings. And, remember, be *honest* with yourself!

1. Are you physically available?

_____ I'm available whenever he needs me. (−10)

_____ I try to schedule a date within a week, if I have no big work commitments. (−5)

_____ I never *ever* cancel a chick night for a guy. (−10)

_____ I am quick to cancel a date, if my girls' club needs me. (−10)

_____ If I'm not available during the next seven days, I feel comfortable canceling something to accommodate him. (+15)

_____ If I'm not available in the next seven days, I think a man should understand that I have other important obligations and wait for me. (−20)

_____ The only reason I can imagine canceling a date is the needs of my children. (+20)

2. Are you emotionally available?

_____ I start many sentences with the words "I feel." (+5)

_____ I am comfortable expressing anger. (+5)

_____ I worry a lot about other people's reactions to my honesty. (−10)

_____ I am always a little coy on the first couple of dates. (−5)

_____ I like a man more when he shares some foible with me. (+10)

_____ I prefer my dates to maintain my fantasy for as long as possible. (−20)

3. Are you already planning to change him?

_____ Only if he's a complete slob. (−10)

_____ I believe men need a woman to help them with fashion. (−10)

_____ If I help him, then he'll do better in his career. (−10)

_____ No, he's perfect. (0)

_____ I can see things that I would like better and I'm going to work on accepting them. (+15)

4. Do you play phone games?

_____ I excel at phone tag, never being "it." (−15)

_____ I always take his call, but am afraid to give him a clear brush-off. (−10)

_____ I don't call back if I'm not interested, hoping he'll get the message. (−20)

_____ I swallow my pride and kindly have "the conversation" to cut him loose. (+15)

5. Are you rewarding bad-boy behavior?

_____ When a gorgeous (or rich) man doesn't like me, I like him more. (−20)

_____ When I feel disrespected, I dump a guy. (−10)

_____ When I feel disrespected, I talk about it to see if I'm overreacting. (+15)

_____ It feels good to be treated with kindness, and I always call those men back first. (+20)

6. Can you wait by the phone and still love yourself?

_____ I keep myself busy with shopping, working, or other men. (–20)

_____ I round up the girls' club and head out on the town. (–15)

_____ I call up a dear girlfriend and cry to her. (+10)

_____ I spend time giving to children or the elderly. (+10)

_____ I take my anxiety to therapy. (+20)

7. Can you pick up the phone to call him?

_____ I don't think women should call men. (–25)

_____ I'm so afraid of rejection that I couldn't bear to call. (–15)

_____ I'll call but only talk if he picks up. I couldn't bear to leave a message that might not be returned. (–15)

_____ If I call, I use a phone where the caller ID is blocked so I won't risk him seeing and avoiding my number. (–15)

_____ I'm not afraid to call. I want to know where we stand. (+20)

_____ I always call guys, a lot. (0)

8. Are you pushing family and friends on him?

_____ I need the approval of my girls' club so he's gotta meet my gang. (–5)

_____ I wouldn't push my mother on any guy. (0)

_____ If he likes me, he must also like my family. (−10)

_____ I can wait a month or two before going public. (+15)

_____ My family's approval is crucial in my choice of a mate. (−20)

9. **Are you aware of how your menstrual cycle can sabotage relationships?**

_____ I am never aware of my cycle. (−10)

_____ I am mostly concerned with PMS. (0)

_____ I pay attention to feelings of jealousy during ovulation. (+10)

10. **Are your parenting skills respectful and empathetic?**

_____ I parent like I was parented because I turned out okay. (−10)

_____ I love to read the latest research on parenting. (+15)

_____ I have taken at least one parenting class. (+20)

_____ I think the problem with kids today is that parents aren't strict enough. (−15)

_____ Kids are pretty resilient. They'll be fine. (−20)

Grading the Five-Date Test

This grade is calculated by adding the scores from The Meeting & Hooking-Up Test (page 86), The First Date Test (page 102), and The Five-Date Test (preceding). Then divide by three.

Exceptional	90–100	A+
Excellent	80–89	A
Very Good	75–79	B+
Good	70–74	B
Satisfactory	65–69	C+
Minimum Pass	60–64	C
Failure	0–59	F

the girlfriend sex test

> What most men desire is a virgin who is a whore.
> EDWARD DAHLBERG, "ON LUST,"
> REASONS OF THE HEART (1965)

What dating book would be complete without at least one chapter devoted to America's greatest pastime—copulation? Sex is everywhere. It is the subject of the hottest magazines, the funniest sitcoms, the biggest hit music, and even the news. It took an international war to knock J.Lo's derrière and Pamela Lee's mammary glands off the newsstands—and that only lasted until the TV networks figured out that a live, prime-time special by Victoria's Secret would be just the thing to chase the public's blues away.

But while sex may be the most talked about subject, complete with myths and falsehoods, it is also riddled with crazy taboos. These are strange times indeed for our sexual identity. This is an era where Britney Spears teaches six-year-olds to show their navels, where sex on the first date is culturally accepted, and where you can also get arrested for tanning topless or, in many states, having fellatio. And worst of all for women is the dark shadow of a sexual double standard that still looms over our beds. I have personally been accused by different men of being frigid and promiscuous in the same week! How confusing is that?

So, I can't tell you how excited I was to get into the heads of men regarding the subject of sex, as purely an impartial interviewer, of course. I wanted to know what they really thought, not what they had whispered to me in dark restaurants. Were they programmed by the boys' club to bring home from a date some locker-room lore? Did they buy into a sexual double standard that put women into one of two categories? Were they feeling pressured to exhibit a male lust for sex, even though they may not want to? Or, is sex really just sex for them, no emotions attached? Basically, I wanted to know what men really wanted from us in terms of sex.

Boy, was I disappointed. Men as a group are as confusing as I suspected. Their values were so diverse that I couldn't make any generalizations about their sexual behavior. One man from Texas told me that he considered a woman to be his girlfriend if she kissed him with an open mouth. A man from California told me that if a woman didn't have sex with him on the first date, he wouldn't proceed further. Others told me they followed the third-date rule with sex, and still others said they liked to play the high school game of sexual baseball, to slow down and heighten the pleasure of their home run. I remind you, these are all married men who eventually found women to match their tastes and settled down with them.

After my phone interviews, I mostly hung up and found myself scratching my head about this subject. What could I tell women? That men were confused? That it is up to us to straighten out their various sexual appetites, putting some on a diet and encouraging others to loosen up a bit? No. That didn't sound right.

Then it hit me. I suddenly realized that I had, indeed, learned a very valuable lesson about sex from my conversations with men, a lesson that we women could really use. The lesson is this: Men all seemed to know what they wanted and stated it clearly, even though different men want different things.

The Male Paradigm

Every man I spoke to had a world view of how sex should be. It was his own personal paradigm and he stuck to it. It doesn't matter to me if the men I spoke with were dishonest about their sexual practices. They may have presented themselves as more adventurous or more restrained than they actually were, although I suspect that most of them walked their own talk.

What was remarkable was the fact that they stated their sexual preferences with such conviction. It was appealing that they seemed to know themselves so well. It was attractive. It even made me want to jump on their bandwagon. Back in my dating days, it was men's belief in their own values that sometimes made me question my own. They always seemed to have the rules down and I wasn't sure I could trust my own feelings.

And how easy it is to bend our own rules when we are being handed so many mixed messages from our culture. If you believe everything you see in women's magazines, pop music, and movies, a problem-free orgasm should conclude every first date. But if you've ever ended a first date with an orgasm, you know that's where all the problems begin. "First of all," according to Los Angeles marriage and family therapist Sheri Meyers Gantman, "Emotional growth seems to freeze at the point of the relationship where sex happens." Because when you add the physical dimension, the body becomes assertive and the psyche becomes protective. Sex leads to a false sense of intimacy that puts our brains in protective mode and leads to nothing but artificial role-playing. No wonder so many feelings get hurt when physical intimacy is rushed.

But back to my point. We are pummeled by so many messages about sex that sticking to our own standards is about as easy as remaining upright during a hurricane. Madonna and Pamela and Britney remind us that our sexual power is paramount in the hunt for a man. Our own good sense tells us that our emotional and intellectual powers are just as valuable. Our body informs us that we have important sexual needs. Our mother may have implanted a little voice in our heads that says good girls don't. Our gynecologist gives us a chat about sexually transmitted diseases. Our high school prom date calls us frigid. The love of our life (ha!) once dumped us because he found out how many men we'd actually slept with. Carrie and the girls from *Sex and the City* show us that a new sexual opportunity is no further away than the next episode. And, after all, there was this new position that you read about in *Cosmo* that you'd love to try out with someone. . . . So, what's a girl to do?

Well, the easiest though most unhealthy route is to set no personal sexual standards or boundaries whatsoever. That will prevent you from going on a major Oreo-bingeing guilt trip should you break your own rules. And so that's what many women do. We depend on men to set the sexual standard. Bad idea. Because, as I've learned, men are products of that same highly sexualized culture as we, except they don't have the punishment of a double standard to stop them from themselves. Most of the men laughed out loud when I asked them if they ever worried about getting a bad reputation. The only bad rap, according to one guy, is to be having too *little* sex. So most of them charge ahead, penis in hand, armed for a battle of the sexes.

Suzanne Blake, a Boston-area personal certified relationship coach (who knew such a thing existed?), has interviewed hundreds of men. She agrees that there is a piece of every man that wants to jump into bed with every date, but it's only a small piece. According to Blake, "Men depend on women for sexual boundaries. Women must pace everything, from how often to see him to how slow to go with sex."

While this sounds like the warning of a mother in the 1950s, there is a new millennium twist. In the fifties, women went slowly to protect their reputations or to prevent pregnancy. Today wise women slow the sexual rush in order to prevent sexually transmitted diseases and to build better emotional intimacy.

The Double Standard: Women's Lousy Luck

In all fairness I need to tell you that I did talk to many men who told me they really were in no hurry to have sex with a date, who claimed they wanted to create some sense of emotional closeness and trust before they went to bed with a woman. I asked some of those men what they would do if the woman really wanted sex early. Every one of them said they would probably take the free sex, anyway, and respect the woman less.

That happened to me once. In one unhappy breakup from a relationship that was short-lived though filled with high hopes, my "boyfriend" actually complained that I had had sex with him too early and then didn't pressure him about monogamy. He said, "I had hoped that at least one of us had some standards." Okay, so he was putting down his own unhealthy behavior, but he was also asking me to be his police officer. No, thank you.

The sexual double standard—the unspoken cultural rule that gives men points for sexual experience and devalues women for having the same sexual experience—is alive and well in America. First of all, let me explain how illogical and mathematically impossible the double standard is. Most men believe that it's okay for them to have sex with many women but it's not okay for women to have sex with many men. But I ask you this: Who are these men sleeping with? Sheep? Over-worked, highly sexed prostitutes? Hardly. A small population of sex workers could never service the randy appetites of a population of baby boomer and Gen-X men. No, those men with high scorecards are having sex with us—peer women in their circle with matching scorecards, only we've been taught to hide our cards. Men and women in our generation are having sex with one another. At about the same rate. Only one study that I found seemed to contradict this slightly. It was a study of the sexual behaviors of teens and young adults and it appeared to show that males in the study were having about 10 percent more sexual encounters than females. But who were they having sex with? When I read further in the study to see if the researchers accounted for this discrepancy, I noticed that the survey did not separate heterosexual and homo-sexual behaviors. In other words, some of these men were probably having sex with one another, and that showed up as a 10 percent blip on the charts.

Yet men subscribe to the fantasy that there are a few women who service most men. They call us sluts, loose, say we've been "passed around." Whatever. It's so silly. But the result could be this frighteningly possible scenario: You go out with a man whom you only kinda like, but it's been a while and, in biologi-cal terms, your ovum is screaming for a shower of sperm. (Fortunately condoms nicely trick Mother Nature into letting our body think we're procreating.) So you go for it. A little pleasure after a long day. The next week, you go out on a hot date with a real boyfriend candidate with whom you want to spend some time building emotional intimacy. The only problem: You're busted if the two guys know each other. The dream man would probably write you off because of the double standard.

Now flip the genders on that same scenario. You found out that your potential dream man had sex with a coworker of yours the week before he met you. Some women might value him more because the mystique of the "player" (or Casanova or Don Juan) can be very seductive. If he's a babe, you might also relish the competition with your coworker. Others would simply move slowly and cautiously. But few would completely write him off. That's the rub of the double standard. It hurts women and it benefits men.

We may own our own real estate, stocks, pension plans, and luxury cars, but if we think we own our own orgasm the way men do, we're disillusioned. So what's the solution? Well, we can pretend that the double standard doesn't exist, living in a virtual state of denial, while we happily copulate with a bevy of boy-toys along the way to finding Mr. Right, but this, as I've shown you, can be risky. A bunch of Mr. Wrongs don't add up to Mr. Right in this culture.

Ya see, we women may not believe in the sexual double standard and may be happy to Madonna our way through that sexual glass ceiling, but we are only half the story in our relationships. Most of the men I spoke with, even the ones who considered themselves to be progressive, were extremely threatened by the thought of women having as much (or more) sex than they. I think it goes back to male/male competition and their own insecurities. They don't want you comparing their assets and skills with those of another man. I suspect this is true because a few of the men I talked to said they would have no problem knowing that their girlfriend was quite sexually active before she came into their lives—as long as they didn't know any of the guys. One man once gave me permission to interview his girlfriend for a paper I was writing about the sex history of unmarried women—as long as he never knew any of the results. Those ancient ideas die hard with some men. Evolution is slow. Our granddaughters may be more fortunate than we. Let's hope so.

Breaking the Sexual Glass Ceiling

I think there is another way to break the glass ceiling and meet our sexual needs without bowing to old-fashioned restrictions on our sexuality. The answer is to examine why we would ever want to have the sexual freedom of men. Most of the men I talked to weren't feeling too "free" themselves.

These men seem shackled with the same kinds of confusion about how to create intimacy, except they didn't have an external code controlling their sexual urge to connect. They didn't fear pregnancy or the loss of their reputations. Most felt that condoms were enough to prevent sexually transmitted diseases. So they simply ingested the message of our culture that says more-sex-is-better and went on with it, not growing toward a greater connectedness. Not learning emotional skills. Just trying to get laid.

Well, ladies, is that the sexual freedom that we want? Whoever said that becoming more like a man would be liberating? With all due respect to the feminist movement, I have a bone to pick. Feminism may have liberated *masculinity* in women—something we took to the workplace and profited from, thank you very much—but it did little to liberate *femininity* in women.

So what does femininity mean when it comes to sex? I certainly don't think it means being a prude or chaste or virginal. But it also doesn't involve substituting physical pleasure for emotional intimacy. That's a male thing. (And bless you men who *have* gotten it together.) If our goal is to create emotional and sexual intimacy within a healthy monogamous relationship, then watering down the milk with a bunch of flings that only satisfy part of our goal is being untrue to ourselves. Just as saving ourselves to preserve our reputation is denying a part of yourself and buying into a patriarchal doctrine.

The answer, I think, is somewhere in between. Feminine sexuality means many things. It is about finding your sexual comfort zone, learning to create trust before sex begins, and learning to say no to preserve your heart rather than your reputation. Feminine sexuality is also conscious sex. Learning to move away from people who hurt is part of being conscious, as is being brave enough to become vulnerable with those we can trust.

Of course, you may be in a stage of life where, for whatever reason, you'd prefer a sex-only relationship. Maybe you're trying to gain some sexual experience. Or maybe you've just come out of a long, emotionally debilitating relationship and you want to get back your sexual self-esteem. Then I say go for it. But I do add a word of caution. The more you attempt to separate the act of sex from the feeling of love, the easier it will be to do so and the more difficult it will be to connect those two worlds again later. We can train our bodies and minds to do almost anything. Triathletes don't feel pain. And sex workers don't fall in love with their clients.

Okay, you knew it was coming. Another personal confession. There was a time in my early thirties when I tasted the sexual freedom that men have. I slept with whoever turned me on. I practiced a kind of serial monogamy that had many repeat patterns. I shared locker-room talk with the best of the boys' club. During that time, more than one man commented to me in amazement that he'd never met a woman before who thought like a man. I liked it when they said that. I thought I had achieved true liberation. I was finally sexually free.

But—and you knew there'd be a *but*—I was no happier. I was not getting closer to anyone. If anything, my romantic liaisons were becoming more distant. More superficial. And my relationships were devoid of trust. That was a deep hole to drag myself up from. If you read *The Boyfriend Test*, you know my story and my journey through motherhood and a new kind of conscious awakening. After it all, I came up with my personal definition of my sexuality. Not what my culture tells me I need or don't need. I now know who I am as a sexual person. I know what kind of sex I like. How often I like it. And, most of all, I know when it's emotionally safe to have sex. (Gulp! I hope so.)

But even if you're still exploring your sexuality, I promise, it does us no good to use our dates as a barometer. We are much better off setting our own standards and sticking to them, even if we are made to feel funny about them sometimes. There is nothing more attractive than a person who believes in himself. And my dating experience has taught me that most thinking, feeling men will compromise to respect you. If they don't, they are a bad match for you and you should move on.

Now part of setting our own sexual standards is taking responsibility for our bodies. And being responsible for our bodies means everything from defining and communicating our sexual needs to taking care of our reproductive health. If we want to be good girlfriend material, we have to be in charge of our own sexuality and, indeed, our own healthy sexual functioning. Female sexual dysfunction is the latest focus of medical research in this post-Viagra era and I'll be talking about it more in this chapter. Count on the fact that men are not mind readers. Nor are they female anatomy experts. And it's not their job to remind us to take our birth control pill, have a Pap smear, or discover orgasm. Despite what early feminists screamed about men's role in birth control, the bottom line is, it's your womb. It's your job to keep low renters out. And it's unfair to put on a man the responsibility of meeting all of our needs. He's got enough to worry about with just keeping his penis erect for us. In fact, as a girlfriend, you'll get bonus points if you can help him do that too!

So go ahead. Take the Girlfriend Sex Test and see how you score.

Are you sexually experienced?

Assuming that you aren't saving yourself for marriage, it's a good idea to experiment at least a little before you shop for a life partner.

Why? Because, according to gynecologist Dr. Lisa Masterson, of Cedar Sinai Hospital in Beverly Hills, California, "The later women have their first experience with intercourse, the higher their rate of sexual dysfunction." Masterson says that she has observed in her practice that if women delay intercourse past their mid-twenties, their rate of sexual dysfunction, ranging from painful coitus to lack of orgasm, skyrockets. On the flip side, though, is the danger of having sex too early, before you are emotionally ready, or when sex is likely to be coercive. Premature sexual activity—when it is coerced or comes as a response to peer pressure, not personal readiness—can lead to an unhealthy pattern of separating the emotional experience from the sexual one. For instance, when a fourteen-year-old girl gets her heart broken and her peers tease her for caring so much, she may just learn to suppress any feelings of love associated with sex. Those are hard lessons to unlearn in adulthood, when intimacy is crucial to successful relationships.

Do you know how to bring yourself to orgasm?
How can you teach him to do it, if you haven't figured it out yourself?

Sex therapists call it being auto-sexual. And if you do practice a degree of auto-sexual behavior—and no, you won't go blind!— you'll be able to explore your sexual self and take charge of your sexuality. It's like playing a fine-tuned instrument. You have to play a smooth melody before you teach him how to strum it. As for how often you masturbate, well, that's up to you and your needs. We're all different, girlfriends. One of my favorite quotes is, "The best thing about masturbation is you don't have to look your best." So, girl, forget that zit on your chin and the stubble on your shin, you are a princess in your own mind. Being a good girlfriend is about knowing yourself first. If you are acquainted with yourself, it'll be much easier to introduce her to a great man.

Are your sexual boundaries consistent?

I swear, the universe offers men 24-hour radio news that broadcasts your inconsistencies. Better stick to one ad campaign.

If you don't want to get caught in the trap of the double standard, then don't waver much from your own rules. It is better to send one clear message out to the universe that will be picked up by the man who is right for you than to fire aimlessly at whoever is at the dinner table that night. Men can sense when you don't know yourself and don't have the ability to stick to your guns. Poor sexual boundaries can also be an indicator that you have poor boundaries in general—a bad risk for the man who wants to couple up with you and create a fortress against the harsh world. Could you protect him? His boundaries? His family secrets? Could you remain faithful when he's off on a business trip and you run into your old boyfriend, the one who dumped you for the prom queen? Believe me, his psyche is thinking about these things as he slides off your panties on a first date when he's heard you're a fifth-date woman. You may even have told him that yourself. So, what does this say about you, that you can't keep your own word?

It also hurts when the reverse happens. You are usually quite generous with your body and then you meet a dream man and decide to play hard to get. Ha! A smart dream man will sniff out this inconsistency and feel pretty angry. You're better off being who you are. He knows what he signed up for. Remember, some of the married men I interviewed had sex with their future wives on the first date. It's not something I recommend—not a good way to build intimacy—but it is a way to be consistent and find a like-minded person.

Finally, if you have had a stint of promiscuity in your past and are bent on finding a better way to bond with someone, you might be pleasantly surprised at how quickly the universe gets the message about the shift in your awareness. The first few men who ask you out may be holdouts from your old advertising campaign, but once you show them who you really are, they become messengers to the rest of the world. I know this sounds kooky because I have no scientific studies to back it up. But I swear this is true because it has worked for me. I do remember one or two slightly uncomfortable dinners where my date quite clearly thought I was still practicing "boys' club" sex, but I kept the conversation on matters of the heart and head, and both guys rose to the occasion, shifting the focus off sexual talk. Not long after, I found myself meeting intelligent men for whom sex was just part of the Wendy-meal, not the entire course. It was refreshing to know that I could subtly control the tone and mutual expectations of the evening. It made the act of getting out of his car at the end of the night a whole lot easier!

When you reach a new resolve inside yourself, it doesn't take long for the world to align with you. If this isn't happening and too many men still consider you the free-milk wagon, then you are probably still ambivalent about your own change.

So, know yourself. Communicate your needs in an honest way. And stick to your guns. That's being sexually consistent.

Are you up to date with your reproductive health checkups?

You can't play a duet if your instrument isn't clean, tuned, and protected.

If only sex were about just showing up. Unfortunately, it also takes lots of preparation. Every woman needs regular gynecological exams, at least annually. There are plenty of good reasons. For one, many life-threatening female cancers are completely asymptomatic—that means you have no symptoms whatsoever until it's too late. You need a Pap smear to detect those. There are also some low-symptomatic forms of vaginitis that can be passed on to men who, without symptoms, can pass it on to other women. If you're a card-carrying member of the girls' club, you'll make sure you're not passing anything around our sorority.

Second, a good GYN is the place to find out about the latest birth control and HIV prevention. From spermicidal foams to diaphragms, condoms, and birth control patches, there are so many options for women today. Being a good potential girlfriend means taking responsibility for all your reproductive health.

Finally, the person to take your sexual questions to is a caring gynecologist, not just your boyfriend who may offer empathy, but probably won't have solutions. If you're having painful intercourse or problems with orgasm, talk to your doctor. If she can't provide you with books and videos to help you, she can probably refer you to an ethical sex therapist who can help educate you.

Do you know how to make sexual requests?
It's all in the delivery, my dear.

First of all, the place to talk about sex is anywhere but the bedroom. If you two are already full-engines-ahead and you suddenly become a traffic cop, giving directions toward a detour, you might find he gets a flat tire. No, my dear, the time to tell him that you like insertion only after plenty of touching and caressing is in the car while you or he can keep nervous eyes focused on the road, in a movie theater while you're both watching a love scene, or in the vegetable department at the supermarket. It is not in the bed.

But all places are still better than no place. Healthy sex involves plenty of talk, some gentle guidance, and some honest expression of boundaries. If you are withholding valuable information about your sexual needs, you are a bad girlfriend bet. This is not the way to a happy long-term monogamous sex life. Believe it or not, there are couples who show up in a sex therapist's office who say they have not orgasmed in a decade. Most sex therapists teach sexual communication as the route to sexual fulfillment.

Learning to make sexual requests is a delicate business. I suggest you begin any statement with a compliment about how much you already enjoy sex with him. Then gently lay on a very specific request such as, "I want you to do it from behind next time. I really like the way that feels and I'm able to feel you deeper." Boom. There it is. A compliment, followed by a clear description of how you feel. You may need to say no more. By the way, if you haven't done it that way with this particular guy before, you might say that you *think* it would feel good, bowing to his double-standard fantasy that if you've never done it with him, you've never done it at all! The other trick is to put your request in terms of a sexual fantasy. For instance, you might disclose that you've been having a fantasy of doing a particular sexual act with him. Remember, even if you're well acquainted with the aforementioned act, doing it with *him* has only been a fantasy thus far.

Your tone of voice is important here. Sexual requests are not demands. They are sweet, seductive revelations about yourself. If you do it right, he'll respond in kind.

Do you understand
male physiology?
Rule number one:
A frenulum is your friend.

I will never forget the strangest assignment I got in graduate
school for psychology. It was to examine a real-life penis
(preferably in the privacy of my own home with a penis of my
own choosing) and simply touch and name about ten specific
parts. Talk about an anatomy lesson! Later on, during class we
were taught the function of each part and the sensitivity level of
each area. At the time I remember thinking that this information would be as valuable to every heterosexual woman as to
psychologists. I mean, my sex-ed classes in high school might
have included a few photos of penises that were received with
gaggles of giggles, but we got no real information about male
sexual function. Or female sexual function, for that matter.

So, great girlfriend prospect, if you've ever had a boyfriend
who understood his own physiology and could also explain it to
you, congratulations! For the rest of us, I recommend buying a
book or two (there are a couple listed in my bibliography) and
brushing up on the subject of male anatomy. After all, you get
bonus points as a girlfriend if you know that the greatest
concentration of nerve endings are on the corona and frenulum
and that these areas are particularly responsive to stimulation.

Do you know how to ask men about what they like?

Direct questions often put guys on the spot if they don't know *your* feelings on the subject.

Part of being a caring, compassionate, empathetic girlfriend is finding out what exactly your man likes. If you depend entirely on reading his body language, you're missing out on a lot of valuable information. The same idea works in reverse, too. If you've ever faked an orgasm during a particular maneuver, you know that that unfruitful maneuver will be his first call from then on. Your body told him it worked so he'll keep it up until you verbally tell him something different.

According to Robert Crooks, Ph.D., and certified sex educator Karla Baur, coauthors of *Our Sexuality,* there are three basic rules for obtaining sexual information from a man. First, don't use yes-or-no questions. If his only possible answer is *yes* or *no,* there is little opportunity for a man to talk about his feelings—which we know is hard to do even on easy subjects like sports. So, questions like "Was it good for you?" are not very helpful.

Second, ask open-ended questions or either-or questions. These will provide lots of opportunity for discussion. Some of the questions that Crooks and Baur have come up with include these:

1. What gives you the most pleasure when we make love?

2. What things about our sexual relationship would you like to change?

3. Am I being gentle enough or am I being too gentle?

4. What are your feelings about oral sex?

5. Would you like to talk now, or would you prefer to wait until another time?

Finally, Crooks and Baur suggest that self-disclosure is the route to opening up a man. Direct questions can put a guy on the spot if he doesn't know what your reaction might be. So, instead of asking if he likes oral sex, simply tell him your feelings on the subject first. Sure, this can be risky. And, yes, you are putting yourself in a vulnerable position. But self-disclosure is also a way to gauge if a man is a good communicator and a way to tell if you should go further. Personal disclosure requires a lot of give and take. If he's doing a lot of taking and not much giving, that is a sign, girlfriend.

Communication before the sexual act can really save a lot of heartache and embarrassment. In the summer after I graduated from high school, I went to a fine arts school some 2,600 miles away from my hometown. I had very little sexual experience at that time and most of it was with a long-standing high school beau. But that relationship was over by graduation. While studying in a little mountain village in the Rockies, I was visited by a young man from back home. He was just passing through and wanted to take me to dinner and, I later learned, back to his hotel room. Over dinner, I thought, what the hell. I'm far from home. I'm unattached. I will take this sexual opportunity. However, no words were spoken on the subject. Bad idea. I wish I had explored all his feelings—even his conflicted ones—before we hit the sack. Well, we had barely gotten down to our underwear when he moaned in a very disappointed tone this little jewel of monologue, "Ohh, Wendy. It's true. It's true. You are easy."

Talk about coitus interruptus! In my embarrassment, I threw on my clothes and marched a mile up a dark mountainside to my dorm. I was completely humiliated. Later I wondered how such awful lies could be spread and who would have spread them. In the end it didn't matter, because in his mind, I was proving high school rumors to be true. The mistake I made was to not fully communicate my sexual intentions: to gain some sexual experience in the world of inexperience that I lived. Instead I probably tried to act cool and experienced, and I obviously fooled him. Communication would have worked better, I think.

Do you practice safer sex?
No sexual act is completely safe but some precautions are a *must* every time.

There's a disturbing statistic that I came across while research-ing this chapter. Although the overall rate of new HIV infections has leveled off in this country, the rate of HIV has been *rising* in teens and young adults who are too young to remember the hundreds of thousands of deaths in the 1980s and early '90s. It seems there is a misguided rumor out there that AIDS is now not a death sentence but a chronic, treatable illness. The good news is that in some cases that is true. But if you think that no one dies of AIDS anymore, you are plumb wrong! And, please know that as women we are at a higher risk of contracting the illness because we are the ones who accept deposits of bodily fluids.

So, here's a crash course in HIV protection: There are four body fluids that carry the HIV virus and there are five doors by which the virus can enter the body. Can you guess what the four fluids are? They are blood, semen, vaginal secretions, and breast milk. And the five entry points? A break in the skin or gums, the vagina, the anus, the penis, and the mouth and stomach. So, how do you prevent AIDS? Simple. Kinda. Put up a barrier against the doors or shut them down completely. With an untested new partner, condoms are in and blow jobs are out.

But do you make that your policy across the board? Or, are you selective with who you choose to be safer with? I know there are all kinds of ways that we might choose to identify a higher risk partner, but the stakes are simply too high for this to be a guessing game. I don't care if your date is a non–drug using, completely heterosexual man who tells you he was celibate for the last decade; you owe it to yourself to doubt some part of the story. It's only your life, ya know.

QUESTION #9

Do you know how to say *no* to sex?
Don't depend on body language and don't ever use the word *no* as foreplay.

Give your words power by using them early on and combining them with body language that sends the same message. Verbal *no*'s that are not accompanied by rejecting body behavior are simply token resistance and often set up a seductive obstacle for the man. And, the earlier you say *no* during the good-bye kisses, the better chance that it will be taken seriously. It does no good to make out in his car for an hour, allowing your body to go into full sexual response mode, and then murmur a dreamy, "No, I shouldn't." Who are you, Scarlett O'Hara begging for Rhett Butler?

I've read many studies on date rape and the most fascinating one focused on rapists' feelings about the kind of invitations they think they are getting from women. Perpetrators almost always blame the victim with that "She wanted it" rationality, so how do we make sure our signals are clear?

The first thing is to avoid putting yourself in an environment that affords your date privacy. Don't go up to his apartment. Don't invite him to yours. Period. I don't care if you've got the coolest chick pad in the universe or if you want to serve him fresh-baked cookies and tea, if you're not sure that you want to have sex with a man, then stick to public venues. Another study of date-rape perpetrators found that there are five factors that, when present in any combination, make a rapist think he is owed sex by a woman. The factors are:

1. The man initiated the date.

2. The man drove and picked up a woman at her place.

3. The man paid for the date.

4. The woman remained in his parked car with him.

5. The woman went to the man's apartment.

Sometimes saying *no* to sex involves changing the old-fashioned script of female passivity. It means taking your own car or offering to split the check. I asked every man I interviewed about what it means to him if a woman offers to split the check on a date. Across the board, the response was some version of "It means I'm not getting laid." I realize that this is a contradiction. Those same behaviors can also be perceived by men as being too aggressive or independent. Such are the complex decisions that women must make. My only directive is to pay attention to your gut and the little voice in your head to help keep yourself safe.

Finally, I heard from way too many men that women use the word *no* as a kind of seductive foreplay. Apparently, it's a way of keeping our reputations intact if we act like we don't really want sex. For many women, *no* really means *yes*.

Well, *stop*! Being good girlfriend material means retaining the power of your *no*. If you say it, mean it, and act accordingly. If you use *no* as foreplay, then you are taking power away from all your fellow girls' club members who may be trying to make their *no*'s heard.

I learned about this awful habit from, of all people, a man. He was a professional basketball player who had undoubtedly been through the NBA's sexual harassment sensitivity training and date-rape program. During some heated foreplay when I happened to murmur an "I'm not sure about this," this man froze. He removed his body from mine, looked me straight in the eye, and said, "We don't go any further until I hear you say *yes*."

I was taken aback. I wasn't even sure if I had meant *no* or even said *no*. But this man showed me that my words have power. He respected my word and was prepared to stop if that is what I wanted. I liked that. We need to train all men to respect our *no*'s and we do it by meaning what we say. The word *no* should never be part of foreplay. Be proud to be a *yes* girl!

Do you know when to say *yes* to sex?
The real question is: Do you trust him?

My firm belief is that sex shouldn't happen until mutual trust is present. But so many women ask me how to know when you can trust a man. Here's my ten-point list of trusting behaviors:

1. He is reliable in terms of showing up and returning calls.

2. He is not pressuring you for sex.

3. He has told you about at least one personal shortcoming.

4. He is happy to meet your friends.

5. He is introducing you to his close circle of friends and/or relatives.

6. He can keep a secret.

7. He is frank about his sexual behavior and mores.

8. He encourages your emotional openness and doesn't change the subject.

9. He is comfortable participating in all kinds of physical touch and stops when you ask him to.

10. He can talk about monogamy and promises that that is what he wants with you.

If a man hits all these points, he is certainly beddable. But before you sail through that list, breezily exclaiming his virtues, stop and ask yourself if you've really investigated all these points. Have you tested him or are you assuming?

And, finally, to truly pass the Girlfriend Sex Test, read that list again, and ask all those questions about yourself. Can you be trusted? One of the men I interviewed told me a story about a date he had soon after his divorce. While he was confiding to her about the emotional trials of his separation, she put a finger to his lips and whispered in a very seductive manner, "Honey, I have great empathy for what you went through, but tonight I just want to f__k." This man was shocked and probably hurt. He couldn't wait to get away from her.

Now go back through my list and think about this woman, so hungry for one kind of intimacy that she forfeited an emotional connection. I think she failed numbers 2, 8, and 10.

What about you? Look at that list and be honest with yourself. Are you good girlfriend material?

The Sex Test
Score Sheet Grade Report

Note: Give yourself 50 points to start out with. Subtract or add points based on your answers below. Choose only one answer per question. Pick the one that best describes your feelings. And, remember, be *honest* with yourself!

1. **Are you sexually experienced?**

_____ I started my sex life between the ages of 14 and 20. (+15)

_____ I began having sex between the ages of 21 and 25. (+5)

_____ I am still a virgin. (0)

_____ I had sex for the first time after the age of 25. (−20)

_____ I had sex before the age of fourteen. (−20)

2. **Do you know how to bring yourself to orgasm?**

_____ Yes, but I don't do it very often. (−10)

_____ No, I have never masturbated. (−20)

_____ Yes, and I enjoy regular masturbation. (+10)

3. **Are your sexual boundaries consistent?**

_____ Always. I know myself and keep to my rules. (+15)

_____ I keep to my rules most of the time. (−15)

_____ I'm a free spirit and go with what feels right. (−25)

4. Are you up to date with your reproductive health checkups?

_____ Yes, I see my gynecologist at least annually and feel comfortable talking to her about anything. (+20)

_____ I go regularly, but I'm a bit shy about asking a lot of questions. (+5)

_____ I go to the gynecologist in a sporadic way, usually when I have a yeast infection. (−10)

_____ I rarely go. (−15)

_____ I never see a gynecologist. (−20)

5. Do you know how to make sexual requests?

_____ I'm totally shy when it comes to talking about sex with a man. (−20)

_____ I can talk about some things but not others. (−10)

_____ I'm pretty open and comfortable talking about my needs. (+15)

_____ I think _all_ I talk about is sex with a man. (−5)

6. **Do you understand male physiology?**

_____ Lord no! That's his department, isn't it? (–20)

_____ I've got the basics down and know how to please a man. (+10)

_____ I've bought a book on the subject, so I feel pretty confident. (+15)

7. **Do you know how to ask men about what they like?**

_____ Yikes. No way. I'm afraid he'll think I know too much. (–15)

_____ I'm practicing this and getting better. (+5)

_____ I love to ask men how I can make the experience better for them. (+15)

8. **Do you practice safer sex?**

_____ I always ask about an AIDS test, always use a condom, and never have unprotected oral sex. (+25)

_____ I use a condom but do engage in unprotected oral sex. (–10)

_____ I use a condom most of the time. (–20)

_____ I sometimes use a condom. (–30)

_____ I rarely use a condom because I don't think I'm at risk. (–50)

9. **Do you know how to say *no* to sex?**

_____ I mostly use body language, but usually get my message across. (−20)

_____ I am sometimes verbally rude. (−15)

_____ I sometimes have sex with people I don't want to because it's easier than saying *no*. (−25)

_____ I pay attention to my needs and use kindness and honesty to set my boundaries. I never do anything I don't want to do. (+20)

10. **Do you know when to say *yes* to sex?**

_____ My intuition has been pretty good at gauging the trustworthiness of a man. (+10)

_____ I'm bad at trusting men, so I like to talk about all the trust issues before having sex. (+15)

_____ I'm hit and miss. Too many times, I trust the wrong person. (−10)

Grading the Sex Test

This grade is calculated by adding the scores from
The Meeting & Hooking-Up Test (page 86), The First-
Date Test (page 102), The Five-Date Test (page 129),
and The Sex Test (preceding). Then divide by four.
How are you faring so far?

Exceptional	90–100	A+
Excellent	80–89	A
Very Good	75–79	B+
Good	70–74	B
Satisfactory	65–69	C+
Minimum Pass	60–64	C
Failure	0–59	F

the ninety- day probation test

Finally. You're here. The homestretch of the race for the title of Girlfriend. Hurrah. Hurrah. You go, girl. Of course, there is still some room for you to falter, so don't count your eggs before they're inseminated, so to speak.

Just like the testy time of the first five dates, the three-month mark is the beginning of another vulnerable time. This is a time when both you and he have made your "friendship" public to your respective world of people (and if you haven't, I ask you to examine why not!) and those strange eyes on your union provide a new social context from which to evaluate your relationship.

There is usually a new kind of pressure as your bevy of girlfriends or clan of relations put their two cents into your head. You may be experiencing some uncomfortable social adjustment as your pack of gal-pals face the fact that they may not be number one in your life for long, or as his boys' club begins to give you some attitude, or as your mother steps up her subtle hints about a church wedding. It's pretty hard to listen to your own voice in the midst of comments like, "Well, if he's the one, he should . . ." But I promise, if you and he are to bond for the long haul, it is crucial that you block out everyone else and focus on your honest self.

Men tell me that at this stage, women either rush commitment or stay in some kind of romantic dating fantasy world that puts too much pressure on to continue to behave like prince charming. At the three-month mark, the glorious façade of perfectly cordial dating life should begin to crumble a tiny bit. Now you're beginning to see the real him and hopefully he's starting to see the real you. Remember, this is how intimacy is created—the ability to stomach his faults *and* stomach the fact that he can see yours. If you're still swallowing a part of yourself in order to impress him, you are creating a system where your authentic self is not a participant. And a relationship like that will not satisfy you in the long run. So, look closely at the questions in this chapter to determine if you're maintaining a fantasy, placing too much emphasis on "he shoulds," or being dishonest with yourself.

Are you still making him jump through hoops to show his interest?

"Don't be a time sink. Don't make unreasonable requests that disrespect a guy's needs."
—Man, 31, Georgia

This is a confusing question for women. While I think it's okay for women to want to be treated with respect at this stage and still be chased a little, there are some women who have so little self-esteem that the adoration of a man is their self-confidence gauge. So, after three months of consistent attention, men tell me that some women still insist that he do all the planning, all the driving, and all the paying. This can be exhausting for a man in today's busy culture.

Now I am not suggesting that you go into a caregiving/plan-making role at this stage (or ever) and take control of his social calendar. You may not be happy with a follow-along puppet for long and, though he may welcome your participation at first, he may later feel too controlled by you. Instead, I simply suggest that you become aware of his needs and offer to make his life somewhat easier. Your message is that his life will be enhanced by you, not surrendered to you.

So, if your apartment is geographically undesirable, offer to meet him at the theater or restaurant if you think he'd like that.

If you sense that he's ready to test out your cocoon, cook a meal for him. Call for theater tickets if he really wants to go, but is just too busy.

Did you notice that every suggestion in the paragraph above was qualified by the words, "if he'd like," "if he's ready," or "if he wants"? The idea here is not to enter his life like a bull in a china shop ready to take over. Instead, it's about being sensitive to his needs and his readiness for your help. That is the hallmark of being a woman—using your intuition well. And, if you're not sure what he's ready for, simply ask him. I promise you, men really appreciate honesty, especially when it helps them figure out what their own needs are.

Have you brought up the subject of money?

"Should I really have to pay for the entire ski trip three months after we're dating?"
—Man, 43, California

Money is one of the greatest indicators of how power is balanced in a relationship, and if the subject is ignored, it can become an enormous underground current that will slowly erode love. The two most common reasons that most couples enter therapy are disagreements over sex and money. And both are metaphors for control issues.

Financial wiz Suze Orman sums it up beautifully in her book (and my personal bible) *The Road to Wealth:* "In the early stages of love, people tend to overlook what they don't like about each other's management of money; the subject seems at once both too petty and too important for discussion. So most people don't mention it at all. If you find yourself in this situation, you are giving money the ultimate power: the power of silence."

First of all, there are no clear rules about how money should be divvied up. Orman is an advocate for a proportional distribution. In other words, if the man has 50 percent more income, he should be paying for about 50 percent more of the expenses. The time to have an open discussion about this arrangement, in my opinion, is at about the three-month stage of dating. That's long enough for him to do some male courting but not long enough for either of you to build up resentment over the fact that one might be paying for more than his or her fair share.

Or you might be on the search for a traditional marital setup in which the man pays for most things; if this is the case, then be prepared to earn your keep by being the CEO of his household and play a passive role in much of the decision-making. Power tends to go where the money is; if you want a strong voice in this relationship, then you've got to pay your fair portion, whether it be in dollars or labor.

The discussion of money should involve an open conversation about your own financial practices and financial goals. Coming to an agreement with him about money might involve some compromises and the ability to stick to that mutually agreed upon arrangement. It's a scary conversation, but one that must be had on the road to intimacy.

One man told me he and a woman broke up after a few months of dating over the cost of a ski trip. He booked the trip and at the last minute asked her to split the hotel with him, which he thought was fair since he would be paying for the airfare, meals, and lift tickets. She was insulted and decided to cancel. He was hurt and stopped calling her.

First of all, a conversation about money should have taken place long before they decided on an expensive ski trip. The woman should have been clear on what her expectations were and saved him the embarrassment of booking a trip he couldn't afford. Then, if they both decided to contribute in some way, they should have planned the trip together. The thing that turned this one event into a relationship buster was the silent power of money. Both partners had expectations that weren't expressed, and ultimately weren't met.

QUESTION #3

Do you know how to deal with the boys' club?

"There are three things that will win me over: food, sex, and impressing my friends."
—Man, 28, France

It sounds hopelessly old-fashioned, but apparently it's true. Their stomach, their penis, and their ego are the tender spots of men that need to be handled with our kid gloves.

I didn't hear a lot from men about how women should fit in with the boys' club, other than staying away or lying low when male bonding is taking place. Really, they do prefer to go to the game with guy friends. And, really, they're not scoping out women there. In fact, they're getting a break from us!

But I did hear many stories about women who embarrassed them in front of their friends. You see, men, in front of other men, want to appear to be king of their castle. They want their woman to be a great hostess and not argumentative. I know this sounds so misogynous, so chauvinistic, so unliberated. But I heard this from really smart, progressive men. Men who change diapers, wear babies in slings, and participate in carpool. Men who cook and men who clean. Even these liberated guys hold a secret desire to feign traditional male dominance in front of their peers. And, say the men I talked to, their peers know this charade is an illusion, but they play along because it feels good.

One man said he was so embarrassed when his girlfriend walked into a room full of his buddies and turned down the volume on the game. (Actually, he didn't say embarrassed. He said "pissed.") He called this the height of rudeness and disrespect. Another told me his girlfriend still wanted to be courted and treated like a princess in front of the guys, which made him feel whipped. Still another said that although his wife always gave him space to be with the guys, he wished that once in awhile she would stay and cook them some nachos.

Now I know, girls, that all this is hard to take. It sounds so traditional. So outdated. But it is the meat of a healthy interdependence. His boys' club is one place where you can give back. If he has to play prince charming for you, you can play Stepford wife once in a while yourself.

Have you uttered the "L" word?

"She can't possibly know me that well before three to six months."
—Man, 37, California

Here's the rub. At this point we may have strong feelings of attraction or even anxiety that feels like love, and we think if we gush forth with the verbiage, he'll reciprocate with a declaration of love for us. But nothing could be further from the truth. That powerful four-letter word is one of the biggest pressures you can put on a man. That's especially true when you say it while he's still doing his dazzling show of courtship. He knows that the person you have fallen in love with is not the real him. Verbal expressions of love given at this stage only make him think he's got to maintain his act for eternity.

I think it's more important to practice nonverbal expressions of love and watch for them in him. A relationship coach told me she coached a woman who waited eight months to say "I love you" to a man, and then had to wait two more months to hear it from him. In the meantime, he programmed her computer, came to family vacations, built her a desk, and bought her flowers. Six months after he finally said, "I love you," he found four more words—"Will you marry me?"

So don't rush the "L" word. It may not bring him closer and may even push him away.

QUESTION #5

Are you able to stomach his faults?

"Some women are great at making a man feel he's not good enough."
—Man, 26, Nevada

I have to say, I was really quite shocked at how many women, according to the perceptions of men, lack self-confidence. That's what judgments of others boil down to. The theory is that if we batter someone's esteem by putting them down, we are inversely bolstering our own self-worth. Here's another enlightening part of that theory. Usually the things we hate most in someone else are the dark things inside ourselves that we aren't ready to look at yet. So if you hate the way he dresses, maybe you really hate your own taste in attire. If you hate his habit of avoiding certain subjects, maybe it's time to ask yourself what subjects you avoid. If you can't stand his friends, maybe you should look at what you really think about your own peer group.

The bigger point here, as it relates to intimacy, is that you shouldn't get trapped in your own projections of him. Psychologists call it lovers' mirroring. To illustrate this phenomenon, think of all your early impressions of him. Were you delighted to have found a soul mate who shared your tastes in food, music, and movies? That's lovers' mirroring at work in both your minds helping you with the myth that this union was meant to be. It is the feeling of "this is fate" that defines lovers' mirroring.

Time to turn on a bright light, honey. He may indeed be the one, but his tastes, as it turns out, aren't *exactly* like yours, and in some areas you guys are at odds. For instance, a few years ago I was trying to be a vegetarian (for ideological reasons) when I met my current man and I was so excited to discover on our first date that he was a veggie-head too (for reasons of taste). We met. We mirrored. We mated. Cut to six years later, after a pregnancy filled with anemia and longings for the taste of a hunk of red meat, and my guy watches me chow down on flesh right before his eyes. He's obviously been able to stomach my "faults" and accept me for who I am. His choice was to decide if this issue was a deal breaker for him and if not, to accept me.

So if you want to be a great girlfriend, you got to reject him or accept him, but to nag him and beat up his self-worth is a fruitless journey.

Are you keeping a backup man?

"Don't use us as a time kill and then break it off when you meet someone else."
—Man, 29, Canada

It seems that the thing men fear most about the backup man scenario is that they are the backup man! This point was hammered home by many of the men I talked to.

"I'm not attracted to women who split their focus between more than one man," said a forty-year-old man from California.

"I hate to feel like I'm being juggled," added a thirty-one-year-old from New Jersey.

The bottom line, according to Wendy's wisdom, is that if you have a backup plan, you'll use it when the going gets rough. By the way, I came by my Wendy wisdom through Wendy experience. I was the queen of juggling men. I would go out with men whom I didn't even like that much just so I could stay busy and be "out there." Ultimately, I had trouble focusing on growing an intimate connection with any of them. And if anyone gave me trouble, I'd just move on to the next.

I have noticed that the directive to "duty-date" is advice given out in some popular dating books. But I beg to differ with some of my sisters in the trenches of the love wars. Unless you have been an agoraphobic for the last century and need some practice in basic social skills, then don't duty-date. In my opinion, it is unfair to mislead a man and take his money if you aren't really interested in him.

I had a conversation on this subject with a single girlfriend recently, who defended the practice by asking, "How do I know if a guy isn't great unless I go out with him? He may not be gorgeous but he may be really smart and funny and I may need an entire dinner to determine that."

To which I responded, "Okay, I'll give you that. Go out with any man whom you kinda like—once!"

If you don't get a charge of adrenaline in your gut when he calls for a second date, then don't waste his time or yours by going out again. If you aren't sure if you like someone enough, then you don't. Period. This man will only ever be your backup man.

QUESTION #7

Are you a high-maintenance woman?
"Her relationship is never enough. She's a gold digger."
—Man, 33, Colorado

When I was designing my research questionnaire, I was eager to have men define the term *high maintenance.* It is an expression I have heard over and over as a friendly warning exchanged between men about a prospective romantic conquest. I assumed that it had always meant *gold digger* and I was partly right. Other definitions included allusions to Barbie Dolls—women who spent too much time maintaining their looks—and women who expected men to be their personal valets.

I focused first on the gold-digger archetype. To further research this particular feline, I rented *Gentlemen Prefer Blondes.* To see Marilyn Monroe playing the quintessential gold digger, belting out "Diamonds Are a Girl's Best Friend" with no remorse, is a lesson in the market value of female sexual power. This woman was hot and she knew her heat had currency. But this was Hollywood of the 1950s, when gold digging had a moral price tag—Marilyn could get many men and many diamonds but she couldn't seem to keep either.

Do I have a complaint about the gold diggers of today? Am I about to moralize? Do I think less of those women who hang out near Wall Street, Aspen, Hollywood, and just about any professional sports locker-room door? Nope. Honey, if you're a ten (or know how to dress like one) and don't want corporate drudgery as a route to financial security, then go for it. Although keep in mind, if your prenup isn't ironclad, your retirement savings plan might take a plunge around the same time your boobs do.

But if you're not one of those, then why are you dating nice guys and asking them to treat you like a Marilyn Monroe? Here's how some of the men I interviewed describe us:

"A high-maintenance woman is not confident with her inner beauty."

"This is any woman who needs new clothing at least once a month, who needs jewelry, and who takes more than twenty minutes to put on makeup."

"A high-maintenance woman is one who is vain, who needs service, who has no respect for how hard it is to come by money."

"She always has to be doing what she wants to do and you always have to attend to her every whim."

"A high-maintenance woman makes her partner feel that he's not good enough."

"A high-maintenance woman is someone who can't find fulfillment in her relationship or in herself."

"These women need a lot of attention. They need to make their peers think they have everything, and they need someone to cater to their every need."

"A high-maintenance woman has to eat at a nice restaurant. She doesn't cook or clean and bitches about not having enough. Picture Peg Bundy."

So I ask you to think long and hard about this. Are you a high-maintenance woman?

Are you letting him see the tiny cracks in your personality that make you so special?

"For all the self-help books and blah, blah, blah, it really comes down to loving yourself."
— Man, 42, Washington, D.C.

As I've already mentioned in this book, being perfect isn't attractive. Neither is liking yourself only as a result of his adoration. Both are extremes of esteem, one too high and one too low. These things put a burden on a man to either live up to the myth of you or to carry you. But I think there is something in between that can pave the road to intimacy. It is the act of loving your whole self, including your deficiencies.

Now that doesn't mean you shouldn't work toward improving yourself—we can all use a little self-improvement. But if you don't bring those self-improvement goals to your romantic table, then you are having a dishonest experience with him and preventing him from being your partner in personal growth. So, whether it's a battle with eating, drinking, lying, or cheating, tell him how hard you are working on yourself. It may even give him the space to come to your aid.

The famous psychologist Carol Gilligan (the first feminist to challenge male-dominated psychoanalytic theory in a big way) wrote about the vicious cycle of female repression in relationships as it relates to esteem. She believes that women in our culture are raised to be cooperative, and as adolescents, for the sake of being nice, girls begin to repress their true feelings. In that mode, we can no longer have truly authentic relationships and this dishonesty triggers a cycle of guilt that pummels our esteem. Gilligan believes that only women who acknowledge their true feelings and express them appropriately stay in healthy relationships with themselves and with others.

I remember testing this theory with one of the great loves of my life. This guy was such a heartthrob to me that I was afraid to ever appear less than perfect in his eyes. I loved to showcase my intellectual skills and my emotional empathy. I entertained him with illuminating notes from this study or that and worked hard to be smart, funny, cool, and, above all, not dysfunctional. Until I had an unexplained anxiety attack one night and phoned him weeping and telling him I was angry at myself for not being able to understand what was going on. I also told him how embar- rassed I was to be showing him this side of me. I felt like a baby, but I had no idea that the baby in me could bring out a kind of paternal consoling in him. I think this guy had always been a bit of a teenager with me because I played the role of good mother.

His advice was great. He told me to shift my lens from psychology to philosophy, and try not to solve my problem through intellectual reasoning. He told me it was okay to be feeling what I was feeling and to respect that the knots in my stomach had some unknown value, even if I would never know why. When I told him I didn't want to feel such discomfort, he laughed and said, "Yah, you and the Romans, and the African slaves, and the Jews."

We laughed together and hugged and eventually made love. When we parted that day, he kissed my face and called me "sweet baby," something that no one had ever done before. By showing him my frailty, I had given him the room to comfort me, something I desperately needed, and by comforting me, he had given me permission to feel. That level of intimacy could never have been achieved if I had kept my anxiety in the closet.

QUESTION #9

Are you able to tell him how much contact you need?

"If I'm not checking in every three to five days, I'm not interested."
—Man, 29, California

By the three-month mark, you are starting to have a real relationship if contact is consistent. Uh oh, I hear the voices of my sisters of anxious attachment. It's as if you are all screaming in unison, "But what is *consistent* contact?"

Is it okay to be hearing from him once a week at this point? What about twice a week? How often should we be calling a man? If we check in every day, will that send him running? Is talking every day at this point too much too soon? Does he really like me if he's still taking eight to eleven days to check in?

Well, ladies, all those questions befuddled me for decades as I stumbled through various unions vacillating between acting cool and acting even cooler, all the while drowning in separation anxiety. Since anxious women tend to be attracted to avoidant men, we have a heck of a time trying to determine if the stress we feel about not seeing or hearing from him enough is our shaky nerves or his bad behavior. Are you ready for the truth? I did find out the answer. It is *both* our nerves and his bad behavior. So, separating the two is virtually impossible.

The only thing we can do is handle our half of the equation, which is to define our needs and state them clearly. And maybe that will have the ancillary benefit of modeling healthy behavior for him. If he sees us being vulnerable and honest, he may learn how to be that way himself.

Recently I had a conversation with a girlfriend who was at wits' end with a man whom she had a giant crush on. He had been in inconsistent contact for about two months. While he never let two full weeks go by without calling, and he did return her phone calls quickly, she was afraid to call too often, for fear of smothering him. So with no clear directive from her he called when he felt like it, about every week or ten days. This was driving her nuts. In fact, as is the pattern with anxious-attaching women (remember, I'm including myself in this brave bunch), the more inconsistent he was, the more she liked him. It was as if her infantile voice were saying, "I'll make Daddy love me this time."

Now my friend is very conscious and aware, so it was easy for me to help her find the double message in her head. One message said, "I'll make him love me. I just have to. I'll die without his love." The other message said, "I am worthy of love. I have needs that are valuable. I am ready to express my needs and have them be met."

So I asked her to tell me what she really wanted from him. That first voice, the betrayed child, was quick to say, "I need him to marry me and never leave me."

We both giggled at the absurdity of such a statement after only six dates in about two months. Then I acknowledged the truth of such a "joke" by telling her that that's exactly what the tiny child inside her needed. "And, furthermore," I assured her, "that child deserves to have that man's unconditional love forever and ever, but now I'd like to talk to the grown-up, logical woman. What would she need to abate her anxiety right now?"

My friend thought for a moment. Then she slowly said, "Well, I guess at this early stage of a relationship, I would feel good if he checked in about twice a week."

Voilà! That was her need. She had defined it as a smart, rational woman, able to separate early life experiences from present trauma. She had come up with a plan that would help her control her abandonment anxiety without engulfing him. The final step for her was to tell him in a kind and straight-forward way. Men like to know what you're feeling. They don't like to be blindsided with passive-aggressive behavior and silly games of playing hard to get. One man once said to me, "Women will tell you everything you need to know about them. You just have to listen." I add one caveat to that: Gentlemen can't hear us if all we give them is silence or happy chitchat.

For the record, men who attach in a secure way may start out with lengthy gaps between their phone calls and dates, but over a period of three to six months, that contact gets more frequent as the gaps slowly close toward a union. And keep in mind that progression from infrequent contact to frequent contact may not happen in an even way. There may be plenty of sputters and slowdowns as he gets comfortable with the idea of seeing you more often, but over the course of six months or so, if you charted it, you'd see a clear pattern of more and more contact. And if that's not happening and you're unhappy about it, he'd prefer that you tell him so.

QUESTION #10

Are you content to be single if he's not the one?

"I hate chicks who will take any guy, no matter who, just so she'll have somebody."

—Man, 26, Texas

The not-so-fun part about defining one's needs and expressing them is dealing with the fact that a man may not be able to meet our needs. And we may have to move on.

Granted, there are a few women out there whose needs are so great that no love partner could ever satisfy them, but those aren't the ones who are reading this book, or any other self-help books, for that matter. Those women can't concentrate on helping themselves because they are too busy judging everyone else. Extremely needy people like to blame others for letting them down. They rarely look for their own piece in the pain.

So, that's not you, girlfriend. Trust me. Your needs are realistic and deserve to be met. The trick is to make your requests in a loving, honest manner, not with the hostility of one who, deep down, is programmed for rejection.

But a time may come when you have to give up hope and cut your losses so you will be free to meet a more satisfying partner. I deliberately used the phrase *give up hope* because I believe too many women cling to hope, nurture a bad relation-ship, and love a man's potential more than the reality of him. Only you will know when it is time to grow without him.

When that happens and you've made a clear resolve within yourself to break it off, men tell me they like a quick, straight-forward phone conversation. Don't make him lose face in a public venue! And they don't want to be blamed. If you need to give a reason, stay on points about yourself and your feelings. He can't argue with your feelings. You own them.

And, please, beg many of the men I talked to, don't use a breakup ruse as a means to bring him closer. That's as bad as using the word *no* as foreplay. It's an underhanded move that has no place in an honest dynamic.

A final word about breaking up: When it comes from his side, make it honorable and respectful. Leave like a gentleman. Don't let your broken heart turn you into a quasi-stalker. If you're having anxiety, take it to an understanding therapist, not the man you hope to win back. For if you are hoping to win him back, there must be enough passage of time for healing to occur.

I'd suggest waiting a few months and, if you know he's not seeing anyone seriously, drop him a card or e-mail, or leave a brief message on his machine. That's all I'll grant you. One more chance at bat. Then, if there is no response from him, you can proudly walk back to the dugout and get ready for a new game with another team.

The Ninety-Day Test
Score Sheet Grade Report

Note: Give yourself 50 points to start out with. Subtract or add points based on your answers below. Choose only one answer per question. Pick the one that best describes your feelings. And, remember, be *honest* with yourself!

1. **Are you still making him jump through hoops to show his interest?**

_____ I like a man to still pay and drive at this stage. (−15)

_____ I'm a babe who loves to take over the plans. (−15)

_____ I ask him how he feels about me doing some of the arrangements. (+15)

_____ I like to see him work for a bit longer. I'm worth it. (−20)

2. **Have you brought up the subject of money?**

_____ I talk about money all the time. It's one of my favorite subjects. (−10)

_____ I'm shy about the money subject, but I
need to know how he spends. (+20)

_____ I think it's way too early for him to know
how much I make or how I spend it. (−15)

3. Do you know how to deal with the boys' club?

_____ I've always had a hard time with the
boys' club. (−10)

_____ I think he shouldn't need to go out with
the boys more than once a month. (−15)

_____ I like to be a part of the boys' club. After
all, I'm a sports fan. (−5)

_____ I tolerate his friends, even cook for them
and don't mind doing the doting-wife
routine in front of them. (+15)

4. Have you uttered the "L" word?

_____ Yes. (−25)

_____ No. (+10)

5. Are you able to stomach his faults?

_____ I accept him completely. (+15)

_____ I nag him a bit too much. (−15)

_____ He drives me crazy and I wish I could
dump him. (−20)

6. Are you keeping a backup man?

_____ I think it's too early for exclusivity. (−5)

_____ I know he's dating, so I do too. (−20)

_____ I like to focus on one man at a time. (+10)

_____ I see my old boyfriend from time to time. (–15)

7. **Are you a high-maintenance woman? (Choose as many of the following as apply to you.)**

_____ A man's financial assets are *very* important to me. (–5)

_____ I take more than 20 minutes to apply makeup. (–5)

_____ I use more than one clothes closet in my apartment (or, if you have a master bedroom, you use the entire closet yourself). (–5)

_____ I hate cooking and know how to make only reservations. (–5)

_____ I hate cleaning and require a maid. (–5)

8. **Are you letting him see the tiny cracks in your personality that make you so special?**

_____ I can't stand to show my faults. (–10)

_____ It's hard, but I try to be honest about my foibles. (+15)

_____ I'm not aware that I have any faults. (–25)

9. **Are you able to tell him how much contact you need?**

_____ No, I'm very good at waiting by the phone and letting him lead. (–10)

_____ I'm not sure how much contact is right at this stage. (–15)

_____ Tell him? I demand that he call more often or he's out! (−20)

_____ I've never done it, but I'm going to try. (+15)

10. Are you content to be single if he's not the one?

_____ I always like to have a boyfriend. (−20)

_____ I am bad at ending a relationship that could have potential down the road. (−25)

_____ I have a great support group of family and friends, so being single is okay for me. (+20)

_____ I sometimes prefer to be single. I get more done and I act more like myself. (−15)

Grading the Ninety-Day Test

This grade is calculated by adding the scores from The Meeting & Hooking-Up Test (page 86), The First-Date Test (page 102), The Five-Date Test (page 129), The Sex Test (page 163), and the Ninety-Day Test (preceding). Then divide by five to get your average score. How did you do?

Exceptional	90–100	**A+**
Excellent	80–89	**A**
Very Good	75–79	**B+**
Good	70–74	**B**
Satisfactory	65–69	**C+**
Minimum Pass	60–64	**C**
Failure	0–59	**F**

relation-ships — a home for the heart

> When we take something personally, we make the assumption that they know what is in our world, and we try to impose our world on their world.
>
> <small>DON MIGUEL RUIZ, *THE FOUR AGREEMENTS* (1997)</small>

In the first chapter of this book, I talked a lot about Attachment Theory, the idea that we are all programmed in the first few years of life to attach to a loved one in a unique way. I hope I also assured you that insecure attachment patterns are not a death sentence for love. In fact, the most effective remedy for insecure or anxious attachment is a trusting relationship.

Many, many studies support this idea. Healthy care-seeking leads to caregiving, which leads to attachment repair. When a guy *doesn't* abandon us and is consistent with his care and attention, our brains can become rewired to find this new model of a relationship fulfilling and attractive. That's the same formula for healing used in a client/therapist relationship. We seek care when we turn up in his or her office constantly (and regular attendance at therapy is our part in the healing process). We receive care for our most infantile needs. Thus, we create a new blueprint for healthy relationships that can be applied to all our relationships. But short of long-term therapy, can another kind of relationship help heal us? I believe it can, as long as it is filled with trust.

I know this sounds a little like a catch-22. You may be asking yourself: How can I find a trusting relationship if I am mistrustful? What if I have anxious or avoidant tendencies? How do I know if my panic is related to my own abandonment issues or his retreating tendencies? How do I know if his smothering love for me is healthfully interdependent or hopelessly dependent? How do I know if the feeling of butterflies in my stomach is love or distress? How do I really know if any man is trustworthy?

I know these questions so well because they have resonated through my own noggin for decades. And the thing I am most clear about is that the answers to these questions aren't as important as the awareness of the puzzle.

This insight came to me out of the blue one morning while I was reaching a crescendo in frustration about how to close this book. You see, I have been stressing about this chapter for months. The final chapter of my first book was a detailed and very personal account of some early life experiences that shaped my later adult choices of romantic partners. The natural place to go with this book would be a dissection of my current relationship, complete with all the lessons, mistakes, and repairs that helped me grow into a better girlfriend. But there are two other people who have rights (and sides) to that story and, unlike the others in this book, I cannot disguise their identities. I am referring, of course, to my partner and our precious daughter. As a public person, I think I have the right to expose myself and accept the consequences but, in good conscience, I am duty bound to protect those whom I love the most. So, there I was, stuck. A word person with no words.

My insight into attachment anxiety continued to grow until the solution to my writing quandary dawned one night. I had rented a Mike Nichols movie called *Wit,* which starred Emma Thompson. Based on the Pulitzer prize–winning play by Margaret Edson, this is a tragic tale of a highly intelligent, emotionally avoidant English professor who never lets down her defenses, until they are ripped away by ovarian cancer. She is 48, single, childless, and prefers to have no visitors at the hospital. As both her body and the medical community betray her, it is her wit about life's ironies and social complexities that sustain her through a torturous trial of experimental therapies. Her rhetorical comments about her situation are poignant, funny, and baffling. In the end, it is the cancer that wins, but only after the woman learns to become dependent on a nurse and regresses to infancy in her relationship with her elderly academic mentor. Finally she had learned to attach and through that, is able to free herself from her body. I cried and cried after watching that brilliant movie (and felt envious of Diane Sawyer, who is married to Mike Nichols, the director of such art). It was all part of the early inkling of my own "aha!" moment.

Then, with the clear morning sun, I had an illuminating conversation with a single girlfriend that honed my new insight. She, like me, is sensitive, smart—and anxious. While she entertained me with the story of her newfound ability to tolerate her own anxiety with a hunky man who was behaving inconsistently, I found myself stuck on the word *tolerate*.

It resonated so strongly with me that I consulted the Oxford dictionary for a complete definition. Here's what I found:

tol´er/ate, verb. Endure, permit (practice, action, person's doing); forbear to judge harshly or rigorously.

Aha! That was it. Healing an attachment injury is a test of our own tolerance. And I don't mean tolerance of him and his behaviors, but tolerance of our own feelings. In other words, can we endure our own discomfort in order to explore change? Can we stay with what's really bothering us, our deepest, most personal fears, and work them through without blaming him?

He, after all, along with his seemingly bad behavior, is the catalyst that has brought forth our cherished, albeit irrational, selves. He is our gift. Men elicit feelings in us—good, bad, and ugly ones. Are we women enough to own up to those feelings and bring them into the light without blame? Or do we prefer to let them fester beneath our awareness, where they can ruin our lives with defensive words and behaviors?

As I write this, something keeps nagging me. It is the thought that a battered woman might read my words about tolerance and think my message is to learn how to tolerate hurtful and dangerous behavior. But nothing could be further from the truth. We are all battered in some way by relationships that reenact our unfulfilled childhood quests. But learning to tolerate our feelings means bringing the puzzle into the light. It means permitting ourselves to suffer with the truth. Can we put feelings of despair and self-hate into the sunlight to see them for what they are worth? That, I believe, is the challenge of being a great girlfriend.

On the phone this morning, I found myself telling that same friend that she and I are the lucky women. We call each other and showcase our anxieties in a pure and authentic way. We support each other in our journeys and try never to judge. And when we do, we make repairs through apology. There are other women out there who may be working so hard to avoid their feelings that they inadvertently sabotage themselves through their defensive reactions to pain. Some women medicate with drugs or hurtful gossip, with food or debt making. In their pain, they may become a workaholic or a manaholic. But it can be a futile line of defense because, like chemotherapy, the remedy can sometimes kill before the ailment does. Remember, I know all these things because I have lived them.

Back in my dating days, I was, at times, a walking character from *Sex and the City.* My shoe shelf and hectic social schedule were testament to the ways I defended myself from feelings. I stayed out too late in the wrong kind of places because I didn't even allow myself to feel fear.

I remember one night around 3:00 A.M. in a dark nightclub, I ran into a man I'd had dinner with a few nights before. He seemed astonished to see me there and told me, "You shouldn't be here. Go home." I just laughed at him, feeling ballsy and brave. Today I know he was right. My lonely bed would have been a more growth-enhancing place.

The message for my final chapter is simple. Let the truth happen. The feelings will lead you to the correct action.

Conflict Often Paves the Road to Truth

There are ways to create healing through a good-enough relationship, and almost all the married men I talked to gave me, unknowingly, a psychological description of healthy growth when they talked about how well their spouses fight. Intimacy is a process of rupture and repair. It is through a system of conflict and resolution that the lightbulb goes on. We see a different side of our partner when he gives us a reaction we hadn't anticipated, and he sees a new side of us when we express our deepest feelings. It is scary and painful, but it works, when it doesn't involve catastrophic damages like name-calling or violence.

Before I offer specific techniques for healthy relationships, I want to remind you about the deep roots of Attachment Theory.

Attachment Is Destiny to Some

In his book *Becoming Attached: First Relationships and How They Shape Our Capacity to Love,* Robert Karen, Ph.D., summarizes the work of the pioneers of Attachment Theory. From the birth of Attachment Theory in the 1950s with such thinkers as John Bowlby came the notion that a trusted person, an attachment figure, offers an infant a secure base to grow on. A child whose needs are met with appropriate attention, affection, and empathic words will grow to trust the world and to trust relationships, and eventually translate that feeling of trust to a romantic partner in adult life. Bowlby believed that the ties to the parent gradually weaken as the child gets older and that the secure base function is slowly shifted to other figures, eventually resting on one's mate.

This tendency of the child to attach in the ways she was attached to happens because the functions of attachment become an internal property of the child herself. The way we attach is a part of us, our own personal blueprint for love. That unique roadmap is created in the first few years of life from the communications and behaviors of both our parents combined with our own interactions with each parent. Then we grow up and meet someone with his or her own unique blueprint for attachment and the work of adult intimacy begins.

The three principal patterns of attachment, first described by Mary Ainsworth and her colleagues in 1971, are reliably identified. The first is a pattern of secure attachment in which the individual is confident that her parent (or attachment figure) will be available, responsive, and helpful. The second is that of anxious resistant attachment in which the individual is uncertain if her parent will be available and because of that uncertainty, is prone to separation anxiety and anxious about exploring the world. The third pattern is an anxious avoidant attachment in which the individual has no confidence that when she seeks care, she will be responded to, and on the contrary, expects rejection. Replace the word *parent* with the word *boyfriend* in all the above descriptions, and you may begin to get an inkling of which category you fit into.

Even Destiny Can Be Repaired

Most fascinating to me are all the studies that examine the repair process of attachment injuries. Poor attachment patterns are not a prescription for a life of solitude. Through the healing power of therapy, of a supportive, securely attached mate, or even of the love of a child, the mysterious internal world of self and other can be transformed. Research supports the idea that insecure attachment patterns are not the eternal destiny of the individual. Change is possible, but it occurs only from within a relationship.

So does it have to be a relationship with a hurtful bad-boy? Hell no, especially if your heartthrob of the moment is only reconfirming your belief that relationships are not trustworthy.

In fact, sometimes the best way to heal is through trying another kind of relationship. But growth can also happen by changing our own patterns within a dynamic—amending the unconscious contract, so to speak.

Studies have been done on the kinds of relationships that can promote changes in attachment patterns and contribute to personality growth. Some good ones include infant-mother attachments, the therapist alliance, and the marital relationship. And the key to healing old attachment injuries is to have a strong affectionate bond with someone, along with the healthy repairs made after disagreements or breakdowns.

Crucial to growth, according to psychiatrist Jerry Lewis, is the presence of ruptures in the positive connections. Since it is impossible for two partners to be completely attuned to each other all the time, ruptures are inevitable in close relationships. Indeed, it is when we bring up our hurt and discuss it with our partners that growth can occur. When a partner with insecure attachment tendencies receives a positive and unexpected reaction from her partner (or child or therapist) and that reaction is repeated in a consistent way, then it is memorized as a new method of attachment. Repair happens.

The Three Ways to Love

All that scientific support boils down to three basic themes of healthy attachment. You gotta learn how to fight well, how to console, and how to be consoled.

Artful conflict was something that many of the men whom I interviewed addressed. They often said they respected their wives because they were fair fighters. Some told me that during the early stages of their relationship, they developed rules together that helped them in their conflicts. No name-calling was a common rule that I heard about. Some people promised each other not to go to bed mad, or not to walk out the door during an argument. Still other men said they got permission from their wives to slam the door, if they needed a cool-down period before they could fight fairly. Whatever the rules, the fact that they were developed together made them fair.

One other married man asked me to remind single women that being in a committed relationship meant accepting the fact that there will be times when you may want to kill each other. But be sure those times will pass and the good will outweigh the bad. Studies on marital stability support his advice. If you have five positive, affectionate interactions for every negative one, your relationship, according to research, is strong enough to withstand the long haul.

The abilities to console and to be consoled are also crucial to a healthy commitment. There is great power in learning to care and be cared for, for a relationship is a home for the heart.

Attachment style can also predict skills in this area as well. To investigate the caregiving process in intimate relationships, one study, from the State University of New York at Buffalo, videotaped couples while one member disclosed a personal problem and the other responded. The ability to request care and be consoled is linked to early attachment patterns in that those who were deemed to have an avoidant attachment style were not very effective in their support-seeking behaviors, and those with an anxious attachment style turned out to have poor caregiving styles.

If you have trouble requesting care, by avoiding it or doing it with hostility, try to remind yourself that by being "needy" you are actually giving someone the pleasure of caring for you. Allowing yourself to be consoled is giving a gift to someone. Make him the hero sometimes and give him the space to love you. If you have trouble offering care and affection during a time of crisis, try to imagine that he is a helpless little infant and you are the all-powerful, all-loving mother. Through giving to him, you will not lose yourself, but gain in power.

The bottom line is that there are no rules in relationships. As put so frankly by one man whom I interviewed, "It's not about 'the man's supposed to' or 'the woman's supposed to.' Forget about all the 'supposed to's.' It concerns only the two people in the bubble."

There are two people in the bubble, but at least six scripts, for both sets of parents are also participating in the direction of your movie—even if they've passed away. The goal is not to get your man to perform the role you have written for him, nor for you to play his feminine heroine. The route to intimacy and real love is lined with lessons of how to write a new script together. And you can't do that if you will be stranded in a romantic fantasy of how it should be, without a leading man.

It is what it is, along with the aches in your stomach and the tears on your pillow. It is what it is, when he doesn't call you back, and the losers call too much. This is exactly how it should be while you are turning on the light, while you are staring at the puzzle and wondering how the pieces fit. Your journey is perfect at this very moment of time, and knowing that will help you cope.

No one lies on their deathbed and wishes they could have worked more. They all have wishes about the relationships in their lives—the things they wished they'd said and the things they wished they'd done. Well, say them and do them now. This is the only way to grow. The puzzle will still win. It still awes me with its power to humble me with more questions than answers. This is all I can tell you for sure: You'll have a better life and a better death if you become aware along the way. Great girlfriends are made that way.

Even today, with all my hard work learning to communicate and connect with others, I still wonder why it can't be easier. Why do my partner and I have to have awfully uncomfortable arguments sometimes? Why do I often have the urge to run away from conflict? Why do I still say the wrong things sometimes? Why can't I be heard and understood all the time? Why does my stomach still knot up when I hear the voice of an old lover whose wounds should long ago have been healed?

Silly me, I remind myself, all I am doing is creating unique opportunities for repair, growth, and awareness. I feel like I am in relationship college right now and not so long ago I was in kindergarten. Will I ever graduate? I don't think so. But I know I'll get better and wiser before I leave my body—and I'll leave behind unfinished emotional work for my daughter. Ha!

She will take that baton and undoubtedly spend a part of her life separating herself from her parents' anxieties. Evolution works that way.

I know that part of my journey has been to repair ancient attachment patterns in my own family. My daughter left my breast and my bed during the first three years of her life, only of her own accord. I held my baby and toddler close, consoling and cajoling her, until she wrestled free from my lap and ventured out as a confident little girl. Today, she is secure, independent, and still intertwined in a romantic love with her parents. I hope that when her heart is broken by her first boyfriend, she will remember who she was in that original cocoon—a completely lovable person.

For that is the ultimate task of great girlfriends, to not lose ourselves in a man, nor to feel completely unloved when some men can't love back. It is the resilient core of self-love that attracts partners and keeps relationships together. And great girlfriends can be created inside ourselves any time of our lives.

Bibliography

Allen, P., Ph.D. *Getting to "I Do"—The Secret to Doing Relationships Right.* New York: Avon Books, 1994.

Blum, D. *Sex on the Brain: The Biological Differences Between Men and Women.* New York: Penguin Books, 1997.

Bowlby, J. *A Secure Base: Parent-Child Attachment and Healthy Human Development.* New York: Basic Books, 1990 reprint edition.

Cattrall, K., and Levinson, M. *Satisfaction: The Art of the Female Orgasm.* New York: Warner Books, 2002.

Crooks, R., and Baur, K. *Our Sexuality,* 7th edition. Pacific Grove, California: Brooks/Cole Publishing Company, 1999.

Fonagy, P. "The Human Genome and the Representational World: The Role of Early Mother-Infant Interaction in Creating an Interpersonal Interpretive Mechanism." *Bulletin of the Menninger Clinic, 65* (2001): 427–48.

George, C., Kaplan, N., and Main, M. *Adult Attachment Interview.* Unpublished manuscript, University of California at Berkeley, 1985.

Hollander, D., Ph.D. *101 Lies Men Tell Women and Why Women Believe Them.* New York: HarperCollins, 1995.

Johnson, S. M., Makinen, J. A., and Millikin, J. W. "Attachment Injuries in Couple Relationships: A New Perspective on Impasses in Couples Therapy." *Journal of Marital and Family Therapy,* 27 (2001):145–55.

Karen, R., Ph.D. *Becoming Attached: First Relationships and How They Shape Our Capacity to Love.* New York: Oxford University Press, 1998.

Leiblum, S. R., and Rosen, R. C. *Principles and Practice of Sex Therapy,* 3d ed. New York: Guilford Press, 2000.

Leidloff, J. *The Continuum Concept.* New York: Perseus Press, 1986.

Lerner, H. G., Ph.D. *The Dance of Anger: A Woman's Guide to Changing the Patterns of Intimate Relationships.* New York: Harper & Row, 1985.

Lewis, J. M. "Repairing the Bond in Important Relationships: A Dynamic for Personality Maturation." *The American Journal of Psychiatry,* 157 (2000): 1375–78.

———. "For Better or for Worse: Interpersonal Relationships and Individual Outcome." *The American Journal of Psychiatry,* 155 (1998): 582–89.

Main, M., Kaplan, N., and Cassidy, J. "Security in Infancy, Childhood, and Adulthood: A Move to the Level of Representation," in I. Bretherton and E. Waters, eds., *Growing Points in Attachment: Theory and Research, Monographs of the Society for Research in Child Develop-mant Serial, 209.* Chicago: University of Chicago Press (1985), 66–104.

Miller, A. *The Drama of the Gifted Child: The Search for the True Self.* New York: Basic Books, 1996.

Orloff, Judith, M. D. *Second Sight,* New York: Warner Books, 1997.

Orman, S. *The Road to Wealth: Everything You Need to Know in Good Times and Bad.* New York: Riverhead Books, 2001.

Rinpoche, S. *The Tibetan Book of Living and Dying.* San Francisco: HarperCollins Publishers, 1994.

Roisman, G. I., Madsen, S. D., Hennighausen, K. H., Sroufe, L. A., and Collins, W. A. "The Coherence of Dyadic Behavior Across Parent-Child and Romantic Relationships as Mediated by the Internalized Representation of Experience." *Attachment & Human Development, 3, no. 2* (2001): 156–72.

Ruiz, D. M., M.D. *The Four Agreements.* San Raphael, California: Amber-Allen Publishing, 1997.

Schwartz, P., Ph.D. *Everything You Know About Love and Sex Is Wrong.* New York: G.P. Putnam's Sons, 2000.

Suomi, S. J. "A Biobehavioral Perspective on Developmental Psychopathology: Excessive Aggression and Serotonergic Dysfunction in Monkeys," in A. J. Samaroff, M. Lewis, and S. Miller, eds., *Handbook of Developmental Psychopathology.* New York: Plenum, (2000), 237–56.

Wieselquist, J., Rusbult, C. E., Foster, C. A. and Agnew, C. R. "Commitment, Pro-Relationship Behavior, and Trust in Close Relationships." *Journal of Personality and Social Psychology, 77,* (1999): 942–66.

Winks, C., and Semans, A. *The New Good Vibrations Guide to Sex.* San Francisco: Cleis Press, 1997.

for more information

If you would like to learn more about Wendy Walsh, her previous book, *The Boyfriend Test,* and *The Girlfriend Test,* please visit WendyLWalsh.com.

about the author

Emmy-winning journalist Wendy L. Walsh holds a B.A. in journalism and a masters degree in psychology. As a relationship expert, she has appeared on many national television shows, including NBC's *The Other Half,* CBS's *The Early Show,* and ABC's *Politically Incorrect with Bill Maher.* As a television journalist, Walsh has anchored, hosted, reported, investigated, written, and produced. Her résumé boasts stints on *Extra,* UPN Channel 13 news in Los Angeles, NBC's *Weekend Today Show,* HBO, Fox, The Learning Channel, and Court TV.

A native of Nova Scotia, Walsh grew up as a "military brat." She earned her B.A. in journalism at Ryerson University in Toronto and worked as a print journalist, contributing to numerous publications.

Walsh relocated to Los Angeles in 1988 to pursue a television career. By 1994 she had become a well-known television news anchor. The O.J. Simpson trial put her further into the limelight as she anchored a nightly trial recap show on UPN called *O.J. Tonight.* It was then that Hollywood took notice. She has appeared in six feature films, including *The Mask, Heat, Cable Guy, Independence Day,* and *Leave It to Beaver.*

Her charity work is centered on improving the lives of children. Soon after the 1992 riots in Los Angeles, she and a group of friends founded L.A. City Camp, an activity program designed to educated and inspire at-risk youth in government housing projects in Watts. Today L.A. City Camp has grown, and its volunteers are still committed to their goal of "Building our future, one child at a time."

She resides in Venice Beach, California, with her boyfriend, an architect, and their four-year-old daughter.

OK ladies, now that you're baggage free
and relationship ready, it's time to put your
potential boyfriends to the test. Find out
how to separate the dream guys from the duds
with Wendy L. Walsh's

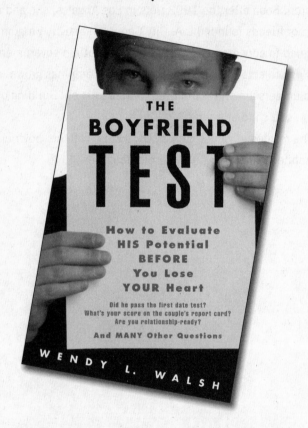

The Boyfriend Test

essential reading for any woman on the
brink of starting a new romance or on the brink
of insanity from her current one!

0-609-80584-3
$12.00 paperback (Canada: $18.00)
Available from Three Rivers Press wherever books are sold.
WWW.RANDOMHOUSE.COM